CW00522007

BETOOTA'S

AUSTRALIA

ABC
Books

BETOOTA'S

AUSTRALIA

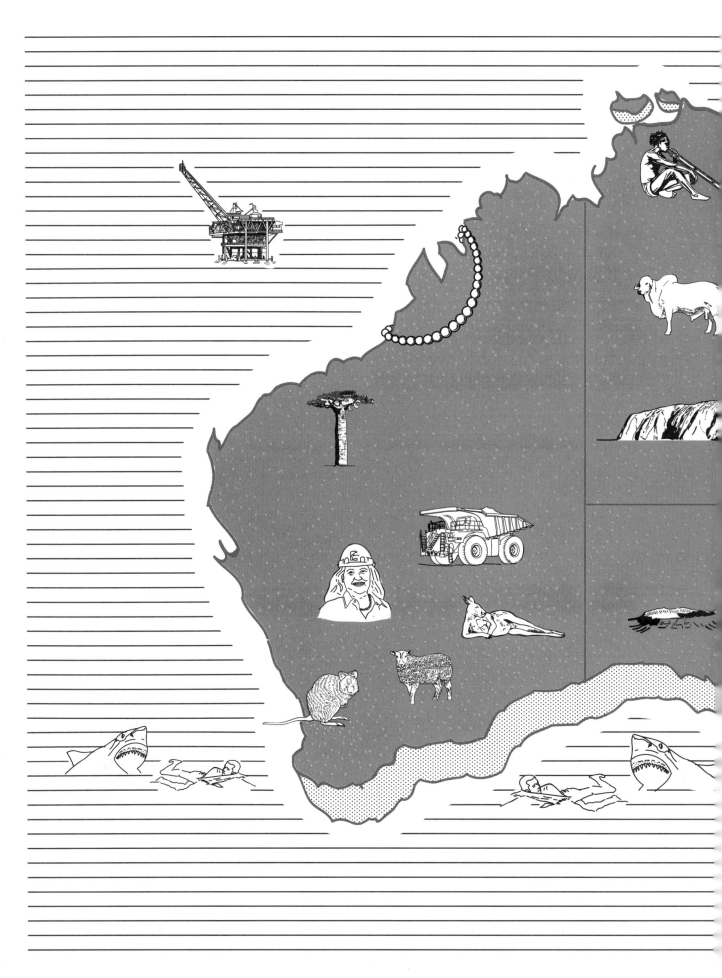

BETOOTA'S AUSTRALIA

Australia's Oldest Newspaper's Guide To The Great Southern Land

BETOOTA,
QLD 4482

Griffith

Our mayor Councillor Keith Carton with
our former state member Robbie Katter MP
discussing the controversial new electoral
boundaries that tore us out of his control.

NOTE FROM THE MAYOR'S DESK

Leaving Betoota for the first time is daunting. It's perfectly OK to feel nervous and concerned about the unknown. But you must do it. It's a rite-of-passage. Some have compared it to the Amish tradition of 'Rumspringa' – whereby the elders of the community give a 'free pass' to their youth to experience what life is like outside their society. They need not return if they don't want to.

As an elder of the wider Betoota community, I extend the same offer to you.

The time has come.

The time has come for you to unhitch your boat from the pier, within the safe harbour of the wider Diamantina Shire, and brave the heavy sea of life that lies past the horizon.

I'm talking, of course, about the regions, cities and people that you'll encounter when you leave this place. Take what you read in this guide as gospel, for countless thousands of young Betootanese have left here for the New World. The stories of their travels and experiences from the land beyond the dunes have shaped this book, which is now in its 11th edition.

While it's important to form your own opinions of the outside world, I also implore you to be prepared for what you may encounter. Read this guide and share whatever knowledge you might gain in your travels by contributing to future editions of this book.

A few short generations ago, we didn't have a tool such as this to aid us on our journey to the more 'cosmopolitan' areas of the country – we were on our own. The only preparation in my day was a healthy amount of curiosity and an overdose of confidence. However, that was then and this is now. This book will be your most loyal companion when you leave Betoota for the first time.

The core message of this guide is to help you understand that Betoota is a unique and special place – but that's something you'll only discover when you leave. Similar to how you'll feel about Australia as a whole, when you feel the desire to travel abroad. Use this guide to help you make sense of what you'll encounter, not to make judgments without seeing the things, meeting the people and eating the food you'll first read about in this book.

So go, young person. Drink from the fountain of good times; let the sun and moon be your only witness. Remember to keep this guide at hand and never forget where you come from.

Good luck and best wishes,

COUNCILLOR KEITH CARTON OAM

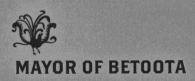

MAYOR OF BETOOTA

ABOUT THE 11TH EDITION

The *Betoota Advocate's Guide to Life Outside*, often shortened to *Betoota's Australia*, is this year in its 100th year of publication.

What was initially created as a handbook guide to city manners and social graces, given to Diamantina youth being sent away to boarding school and our young ringers heading to Brisbane for the Royal Show, has now become an award-winning categorised index of life outside our town.

As a small and independent regional newspaper from Far-West Queensland, we pride ourselves on reporting fair and just news, with an authenticity that rivals only the salt on the sunburnt earth that surrounds us here in the Queensland Channel Country.

Established in the mid-1800s, we are arguably Australia's oldest newspaper and have always taken pride in our ability to walk in both worlds: regional and metropolitan news. In recent times, our popularity has grown immensely as the result of a bold move to create an online revival for our publication. ☞

Above: Clancy Overell (left) and Errol Parker, editors of *The Betoota Advocate*. Australia's oldest newspaper.

While our humble town's population is 'officially' listed as zero, it's commonly acknowledged that a majority of our residents have avoided all forms of census and documentation since the Y2K Bug.

It is because of our comprehensive understanding of life outside the Shire that we have taken it upon ourselves to help equip our locals with the dos and don'ts of the big smoke.

Australia is a vast continent, varying in landscape, industry and tribes – be they Indigenous or adventitious. For our community, the complexities of life on the coast or life further south is just about as foreign as a life abroad.

It is for this reason that the book you're holding, which marks the 11th edition of the guide, has become popular with unskilled European labourers, who are sent to our district in a program that helps them learn about our country's ways and extend their visas long enough to enjoy another summer in Bondi Junction.

Through our town's visiting back-packers, word of our guide has spread across the country. Now the publication is in great demand among different immigration services and tourism agencies all over Australia.

In fact, our comprehensive guide to contemporary Australian culture for the small-town kid has translated well right across the country. People from all walks of life use Betoota's Australia to navigate their way through the giant cities, towns and personalities that one comes in contact with while travelling the Great Southern Land.

Australia's oldest newspaper, *The Betoota Advocate* has worked tirelessly to describe the people, the places, the politics, the cultural rituals and the language that make up this great land. And, for the centenary celebration of the guide, we have decided to share it with all Australians through a nationwide print run, orchestrated through the News Limited branch of the public broadcaster, ABC Books HarperCollins.

CLANCY OVERELL AND ERROL PARKER, EDITORS

BET

INL

AUS

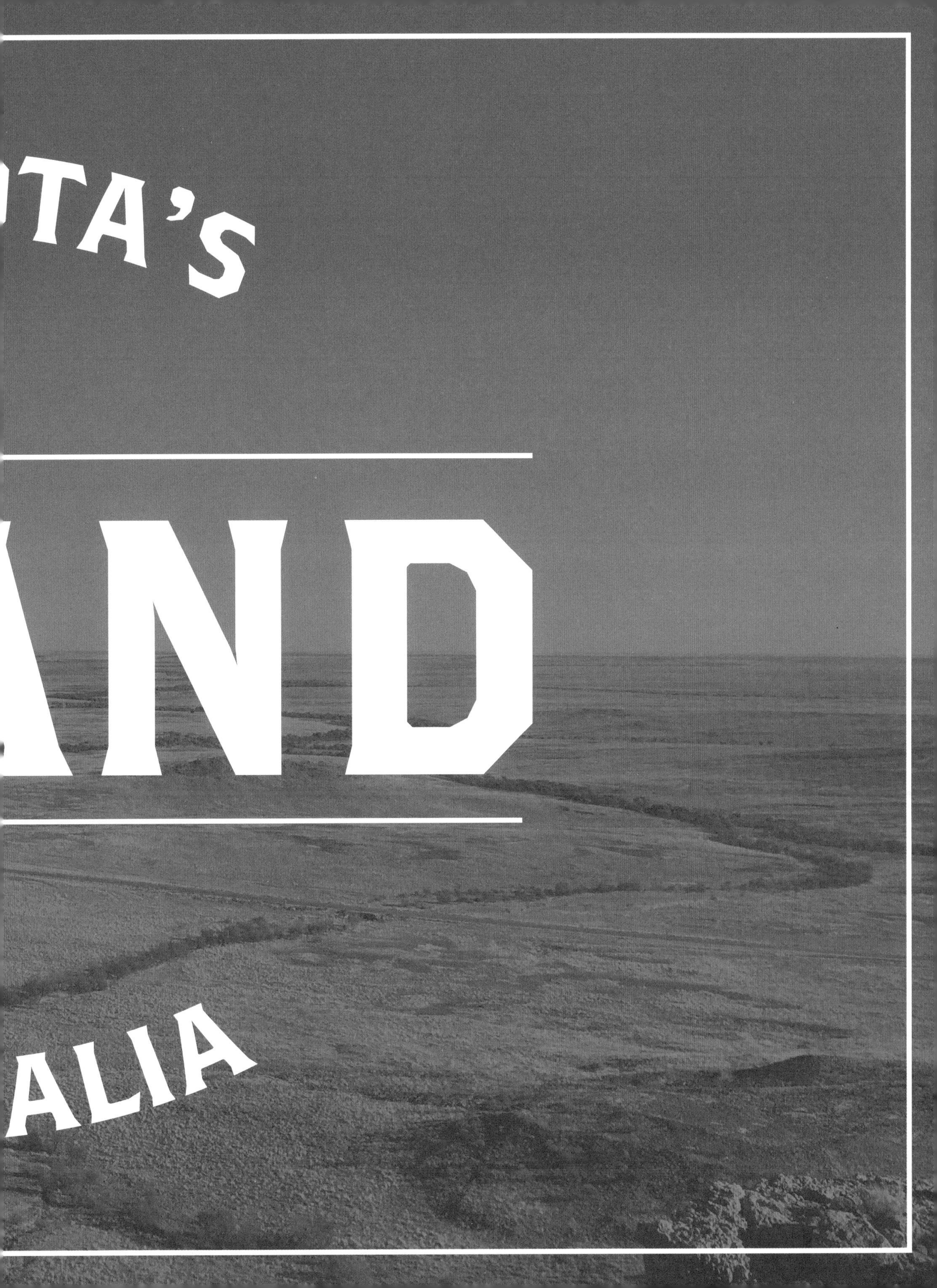
TA’S
AND
ALIA

THE REGIONS

PLACES TO SEE

Outback Qld

Bush NSW

Regional Victoria

The Top End

OUTBACK

QUEENSLAND

'On the outer Barcoo where the churches are few, And men of religion are scanty ...' – Banjo Paterson, 'A Bush Christening', 1893

NOTABLE PEOPLE

The bloke who plays Alf on 'Home and Away'

Deborah Mailman ('Secret Life Of Us', TV)

Errol Parker (Betoota Advocate)

Clancy Overell (Betoota Advocate)

Artie Beetson (rugby league)

Quentin Bryce (former Governor-General)

Darren Lockyer (rugby league)

Greg Norman (golfwear entrepreneur)

Pat Rafter (Bonds Model)

OUTBACK Qld

NOTABLE TOWNS

1. Betoota
2. Birdsville
3. Cunnamulla
4. Mt Isa
5. Charleville
6. Longreach
7. Blackall
8. Roma
9. Mitchell
10. St George
11. Yaraka
12. Barcaldine

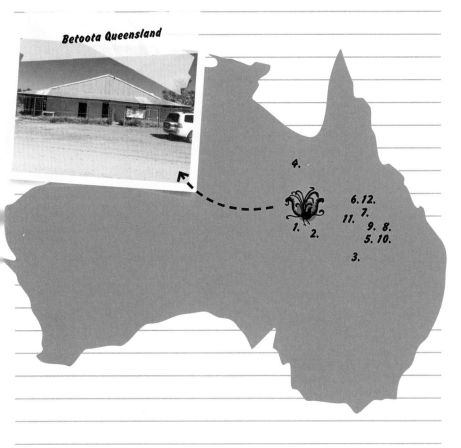

Betoota Queensland

Over the last two hundred years, Outback Queensland has been responsible for some of Australia's biggest exports – lamb, beef, wool, grain and commercial aeroplane flights.

The western regions of Queensland are renowned for their remarkable contribution to contemporary Australia. Qantas (Queensland and Northern Territory Air Service) was formed in Longreach, the ALP (Australian Labor Party) was formed in Barcaldine, and the country's largest independent newspaper hails from the eye of the Diamantina Shire, Betoota.

With unique style, language and culture, South-West and Central-West Queensland are themselves republics within the already succession-ready northern state.

The remoteness of townships and the distances between them have resulted in a rare show of unity between all three demographics that make up the population. Unlike the more tribal southern towns, Outback Queensland was the first region to allow blacks on the council – Catholics followed soon after.

The western regions of Queensland are often drought-stricken and rely heavily upon bore water from the Great Artesian Basin, which is the largest and deepest artesian basin in the world, stretching over 1,700,000 square kilometres.

Common held theories suggest that the Artesian Basin is the leading cause of Western Queensland's success in producing such high-performing footballers. As the minerals found in groundwater may be responsible for ☞

THE OUTBACK
LANDMARKS

1. Longreach Stockman's Hall of Fame

2. The Winton Dinosaur Footprint

3. The Lyceum Hotel

4. Kangaroo statue in Charleville

5. The Mitchell Hot Baths

6. Barcaldine Tree of Knowledge

7. Kidman Tree of Knowledge

Above: The iconic Dinosaur footprints of Winton, Far-West Qld. Left: Deputy Prime Minister Barnaby Joyce sporting a black eye after a run-in with the locals at the Lyceum Hotel in Longreach.

the hardened make of athlete in the Outback.

However, with technological leaps in coal seam gas drilling and hydraulic fracturing, the region's water supply is now also a handy tool for natural resource extraction. Residents say they are growing used to the taste of benzene, toluene, ethyl-benzene and xylene.

Australian Deputy Prime Minister Barnaby Joyce says his time as an accountant in the one-horse town of Dirranbandi is the sole reason he was able to reach the lofty heights of the National Party as quickly as he did.

Right: Clancy Overell (left) and Errol Parker with David Littleproud, Federal member.

Joyce believes his Les Norton-brand of aggressive – sometimes even violent – problem-solving made him an instant hit in the square and considered halls of Canberra.

In a true example of taking the boy out of the bush but being unable to take the bush out of the boy, the Deputy Prime Minister was quick to the knuckle during a visit to a notorious pub in Outback Queensland, while on the 2016 campaign trail when he was allegedly punching on with patrons.

Built in 1896, the Lyceum Hotel in Longreach is internationally known for its rowdy atmosphere and ability to put on a good barny, even on weeknights. It seems the fact that the second-highest-ranking politician in the country was visiting didn't change much.

Speaking to *The Betoota Advocate* on his way back home to Tamworth, Mr Joyce refuted claims that he had been 'run out of town' – despite the fact he was sporting an obvious black eye.

'It was just like any other night in Longreach,' said the Deputy Prime Minister between sips from a 1.2 litre Frozen Coke he had picked up at the Roma McDonald's.

'Sometimes these things just happen.'

Surprisingly, despite all of Outback Queensland's rural sensibilities and God-fearing conservatism, the area is also home to Australia's version of Area 51.

Much like the American CIA's southern Nevada airport, known as 'Roswell' or 'Area 51' – the far-west Queensland town of Boulia has for many years been embroiled in conspiracy theories related to the

Right: Clancy Overell (left) and Errol Parker with David Littleproud, Federal member.

MR JOYCE REFUTED CLAIMS THAT HE HAD BEEN 'RUN OUT OF TOWN'.

supernatural phenomenon of 'Min Min lights'.

First reported by travelling stockmen in the early 1900s, stories about the lights can be found in Aboriginal myths pre-dating white fellas.

Min Min lights, described as sparkly, dim, disc-shaped lights that appear to hover just above the horizon, have made the Queensland Channel Country a well-known region in the international tinfoil-hat community.

Diamantina Shire Desert

Quilpie Races

Quilpie Race Course

adtrain out the front of the Betoota Hotel

Betoota Race Track

Mount Leonard Station at sunset

Windorah Solar Farm

BUSH NSW

'If you know Bourke, you know Australia.' – Henry Lawson, 1910

NOTABLE PEOPLE

George Rose (Walgett rugby league)

Glenn McGrath (cricket)

Margaret Vyner (actress)

Beau Robinson (rugby union)

Windradyne (Aboriginal warrior)

Judith Wright (poet)

Fred Hollows (eye doctor, buried in Bourke)

Lisa Keightley (first female cricketer to score a century at Lord's)

Tom Tilley (triple j presenter, well-known communist)

Ken Sutcliffe (male model, news presenter)

The NSW Bush represents one of the most diverse rural regions in Australia – in industry, landscape, demographics and culture.

From the blueblood plains of New England to the Victorian border, the people live according to their surroundings and employment.

While the agriculture ranges from cherries in Young, beef in Narromine and cotton in Moree, places like Mudgee and Muswellbrook have achieved what no other towns have done in the world, dividing their water, land and workforce between award-winning wineries and sprawling open-cut coal mines.

This unique pick of foolproof non-agricultural industries has given these districts the chance to create communities that aren't built around staffing high-security prisons – also common on the western side of the Great Dividing Range.

BUSH NSW
NOTABLE TOWNS

1. Goulburn
2. Lithgow
3. Bathurst
4. Orange
5. Mudgee
6. Tamworth
7. Armidale
8. Dubbo
9. Cootamundra
10. Wagga Wagga
11. Walgett
12. Broken Hill
13. Wilcannia
14. Bourke

Dubbo's Western Plains Zoo, home to over 1000 different species of wildlife. Also briefly home to bushranger Malcolm Naden during his seven-year run from the law.

The 'Three Sisters' rock formation in the Blue Mountains, arguably the unofficial gateway to Bush NSW.

Much like these towns and others further north in the Hunter Valley with their endless winery tours, the sleepy village of Bathurst at the foothills of the Blue Mountains has also become a household name for drunken tourism – hosting tens of thousands of motor enthusiasts at their annual 1000-kilometre Supercar race on the internationally renowned Mt Panorama racetrack each year.

But it isn't all just grog, handcuffs and meat trays. With the largest number of regional universities in the country, the NSW Bush is also a prolific contributor to Australian

THE NSW BUSH IS ALSO A PROLIFIC CONTRIBUTOR TO AUSTRALIAN SCIENCES, RESEARCH AND MARIJUANA USE.

BUSH NSW LANDMARKS

1. *Mount Panorama Circuit, Bathurst*
2. *The Dish, Parkes Observatory*
3. *Bradman's birthplace, Cootamundra*
4. *The Big Golden Guitar, Tamworth*
5. *Silverton Hotel*
6. *Lithgow Correctional Centre*
7. *Goulburn Correctional Centre*
8. *Wellington Correctional Centre*
9. *Bathurst Correctional Complex*
10. *Oberon Correctional Centre*
11. *Brewarrina Correctional Centre*
12. *Moree Correctional Centre*

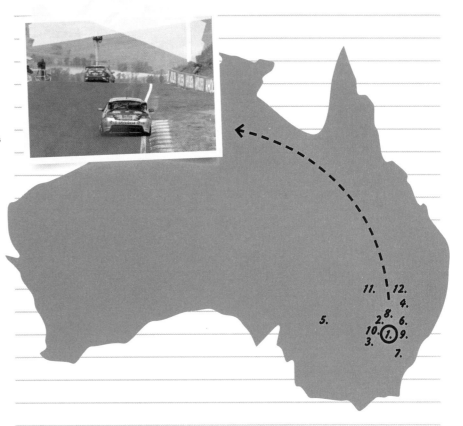

sciences, research and marijuana use.

This part of the world is recognised as a place of interest by overseas governments, whether it's the radio telescope dish in Parkes that was solicited by NASA to help broadcast the moon landings, or the ISIS-sympathising rocket scientists living in Young, to whom the FBI suggested NSW police pay a visit.

Like the rest of the Australian scrub, Bush NSW towns are held together by the mortar of club sport. And, due to the sheer size of regional NSW, they cover all codes – from Wayne Carey to the Mortimer brothers. The Riverina town of Wagga Wagga is considered to be the official divide between AFL and the rugby codes.

As a population sample, Wagga Wagga is far more representative of this country than you'll find in the halls of Parliament House. If you've been to Wagga, you've been to Australia.

Further west down the river, however, the demographics change dramatically when you reach Griffith.

This iconic 'wine region' of Outback NSW is known for its interesting European flavour, which stems from the fact that 80 per cent of the town claims either Sicilian or Calabrian ancestry.

The hard work of these rural migrant families has resulted in Griffith having a monopoly on Australia's fruit markets, wine exports and orchard fertilisers … if you know what we're saying.

Above: The main drag of Wagga Wagga, NSW, a town so nice they named it twice.

COME AND CRUSH TINS AT THE
BETOOTA
CAMEL RACES

REGIONAL
VICTORIA

'All your stuff is hot to touch, even the back of the truck was off the back of the truck.' – Adam Briggs ('Sheplife', 2014)

NOTABLE PEOPLE

Nick Cave (musician)

Reginald Ansett (founder of Ansett Airways)

Sidney Myer (founder of Myer department stores)

Frank McEncroe (inventor of the Chiko Roll)

Adam Briggs (rapper)

Jason Akermanis (former Victorian Football player)

Diabetes (Ararat)

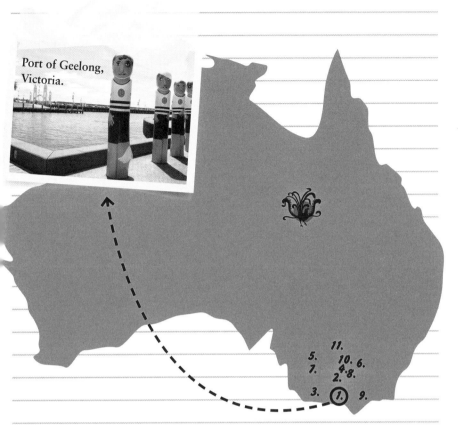

Port of Geelong, Victoria.

REGIONAL VIC

NOTABLE TOWNS

1. Geelong
2. Ballarat
3. Warrnambool
4. Bendigo
5. Mildura
6. Wodonga
7. Horsham
8. Shepparton
9. Sale
10. Wangaratta
11. Echuca

Home to bushrangers, goldmines and the wild frontier, regional Victoria is the nation's Garden of Eden when it comes to history and culture.

Though it was once the epicentre of Australian commerce and trade, regional Victoria is now a tourism mecca that attracts visitors in the millions. Whether you're a casual weekender or a greyest nomad – there's something for everyone in the Victorian bush.

Recently, as you may have seen in the news, the region is trying to combat skyrocketing rates of methamphetamine addiction and obesity – as are most other regional areas in Australia.

However, don't let anybody tell you that any other region beats rural Victoria in those figures. Rural Victorians are

The body armour of iconic bushranger Ned Kelly, who is often associated with Australian nationalism, despite being an Irishman who hated the Australian government.

categorically and comprehensively the biggest Australian users of methamphetamines. Scientists have concluded that the amount of ice in the region is almost enough to reverse global warming.

In saying that, this particular section of countryside has also given birth to some of the nation's most important cultural and societal identifiers.

The Battle of the Eureka Stockade, in 1854, was one of the first instances that an Australian identity came to the forefront, when a group of goldminers in Ballarat revolted ☞

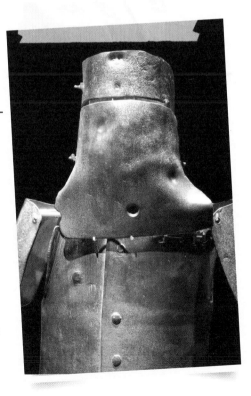

REGIONAL VIC
LANDMARKS

1. The Big Arch of Victory (Ballarat)

2. The Big Earthworm (Bass)

3. The Big Koala (Dadswells Bridge)

4. The Big Milkshake (Warrnambool)

5. The Big Murray Cod (Swan Hill)

6. The Big Ned Kelly (Glenrowan)

7. The Big Root (Nowa Nowa)

8. The Big Wool Bales (Hamilton)

against the colonial forces of the British Empire. The rebellion, and what it stood for, is still used as a *casus belli* by Aussie patriots protesting against foreigners and people that don't look like them.

When gold was king, there was no wealthier region than regional Victoria.

While some would argue that Central-West New South Wales had a more significant gold rush, they are wrong.

For a time, migrant workers and prospectors littered the hills and valleys of regional Victoria, like kangaroos litter the highways and laneways of the Warrego. To put it simply, there were more people in regional Victoria than roos you could bounce off a bullbar at dusk between Bourke and Cunnamulla.

THE REGION IS TRYING TO COMBAT SKYROCKETING RATES OF METHAMPHETAMINE ADDICTION AND OBESITY.

Like most good things, however, they come to an end.

The gold rush in regional Victoria ended in the twilight years of the 19th century and with it ended the region's period of wealth. The widespread opportunity that existed in the gold rush years gave way to the agricultural era – when the landowning class rode on the sheep's back until that good thing came to its inevitable end, too.

Nowadays, the type of Australian you'll most likely encounter in this

Regional Victoria, as it was during the gold rush ...

... and Regional Victoria as it is now, during the crystal rush.

part of the country is the humble battler – hardworking, stoic and likely addicted to something or other – whether that be food, sugar, caffeine or an illicit substance.

It's a sad reflection on the economic and social prospects of the area. A lot of the youth from the region leave for those reasons. Without jobs, good times and responsibility, life can decay into what you've come to learn about regional Victoria.

Which is why our region hasn't suffered the same fate.

There are jobs, good times, as well as the unabridged responsibility that comes from working in gas, mining and agriculture.

So take heed of these words and keep your wits about you when visiting rural Victoria. Enjoy her fruits but try not to break the skin, because what lies beneath is something truly horrifying.

THE
TOP END

'It is majestic ... There is certainly is no other place I would rather call home.' – Nova Peris OAM, maiden speech to Parliament, 2013

NOTABLE PEOPLE

Damien Martyn (cricketer)

David Gulpilil (actor, dancer)

Cadel Evans (former Tour de France winner)

Leisel Jones (former Olympic swimmer)

Jessica Mauboy (singer, actor)

Tex Perkins (former frontman of The Cruel Sea)

Nova Peris (former Olympian, former politician)

Ben Barba (rugby league player)

Many agree that Daryl Somers and some Big City ad agency besmirched Barcroft Boake's description of the Top End when they used the term 'Never Never' in a 1994 advertising campaign for the Territory – they say it wasn't true to the poem's meaning.

The *Cambridge History of Australian Literature* describes 'Where the Dead Men Lie', first published in *The Bulletin* in 1891, 'as by far the bleakest poetic vision' of the Australian landscape because it evokes 'a haunted frontier'.

Daryl Somers, by any stretch of the imagination, does not ooze that image.

That single ad campaign has helped to define what the Top End is and what is has become in recent times.

It is similar, yet eerily different, to Outback Queensland and the NSW Bush. The distances become longer, ☞

The pristine waters of Darwin, Northern Territory.

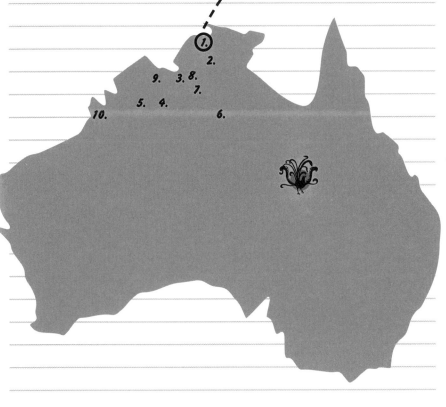

TOP END
NOTABLE TOWNS

1. Darwin
2. Katherine
3. Kununurra
4. Halls Creek
5. Fitzroy Crossing
6. Tennant Creek
7. Top Springs
8. Timber Creek
9. Wyndham
10. Broome

Above: The iconic red dirt of Australia's Top End, well known for its ability to make inner-city 4WDs look rugged.

the country dies off and you're often left with just a road and the horizon for company. It's definitely a land of two worlds.

For those who've grown up and lived there, the glossy magazine ads and friendly faces on the TV screen that beckon people to visit the Top End are few and far between. Yes, they're there, but they won't be there when you stop in Timber Creek and ask for directions.

But for those who travel all the way up there, above the Tropic of Capricorn, it seems like a different country. The people, the heat, the noise at night and the air. It all looks like what they thought it would. It's what they were promised. But Barcroft Boake made it clear that, up in the Top End, nothing is for certain except heat and death.

The people you'll encounter in the hot country aren't dissimilar from those you'd find around town, save for a few small things. But that's not a salient issue. Top Enders speak with the slow, tempered drawl that many of the elder members of our community speak – Interior Australian English.

When travelling abroad from the wider Diamantina, this is where you'll feel most at home. Sort of how an Irishman feels more at home in Scotland than he would England. Bound by a mutual loathing.

However, one of those small differences comes in the form of sport.

TOP ENDERS SPEAK WITH THE SLOW, TEMPERED DRAWL THAT MANY OF THE ELDER MEMBERS OF OUR COMMUNITY SPEAK – INTERIOR AUSTRALIAN ENGLISH.

Though Darwin has produced one of the finest batsman this country has ever seen in Damien Martyn, that's where the similarities with Betoota end. Victorian Rules Football has taken hold in the Top Country, with little sign of it loosening its grip. Some of the greatest players of the modern game have called the Top End home. Watching a Victorian Rules match in the Top End should be on your bucket list.

Treat those you meet up there as your own, but still keep them at arm's length.

TOP END LANDMARKS

1. Kakadu National Park
2. Gove Peninsula
3. Top Springs Hotel (Top Springs)
4. Newcastle Waters Station
5. Hotel Kununurra (Kununurra)
6. Lake Argyle
7. The Crossing Inn (Fitzroy Crossing)
8. Hoochery Distillery (Kununurra)
9. Eighty Mile Beach

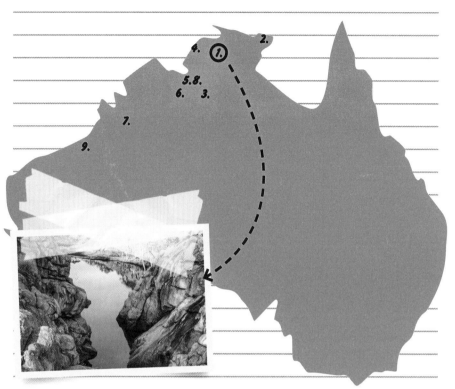

THE LOCALS

NOTABLE TYPES

The Townie

The First Australians

The Busted Cocky

THE TOWNIE

OFTEN FOUND

The Hume (Vic)

New England (NSW)

Central West (NSW)

Maranoa (Qld)

Mackay (Qld)

The Riverland (SA)

Kalgoorlie (WA)

ALSO KNOWN AS

Trouble

The Local Crowd

Cornfeds

LIKES

American country music

American gangster rap music

Holden Commodores

White dress shoes

DISLIKES

City slickers

Cowboy hats that aren't black

Coppers

The Townie is the forgotten backbone of the Outback – the regional Australian who lives in town. They don't work the land, but they are partial to going out bush with the spotties on and blasting a few roos.

With a penchant for rodeos and Lee Kernaghan, the Townie is arguably more country than the Australian Cattleman.

However, unlike the softly spoken Bush Cocky, the Townie is well known for his outspokenness and vocal hatred of authority figures – especially coppers – and seckos. This is because their idea of fun is often at odds with the local 'Terry Tough c—t' wearing a badge.

Rude haircuts, motorbike stunts and a good scrap are commonplace in the streets and pubs of Australian small towns, especially when the solicitor's sons come back from their private boarding school for the holidays.

Their fashion sense is strongly based around hip-hop-themed streetwear and extreme sports brands. Townie kids are also renowned for their ability to jump fences and pinch smokes from their old man.

When it comes to ethnicity, Townies are predominantly Caucasian or ginger-haired blackfellas, although, the country's many regional Chinese and Thai restaurant owners are also well known for producing first-generation Townie kids.

It is believed that Australia's female population of Townies are the sole reason that P!nk tours Australia every 18 months.

When it comes to the small-town economy, it's the Townie population that fills our showgrounds, pubs and high schools in the bush. While we like to think that our great Outback is made up of Hugh Jackman lookalikes on horseback, the reality is, most regional Australians are wearing metallic Fox motocross shirts.

Cultural traditions appear to vary between states, but the most widely accepted form of initiation into adulthood as a Townie is proving one's ability to do backflips from the 10-metre diving board at the local public pool.

THE FIRST AUSTRALIANS

ALSO KNOWN AS

Aboriginal and Torres Strait
Islander Identifying Peoples

Blackfellas

LIKES

Maintaining culture

Slim Dusty

Worcestershire Sauce

YouTube punch-ons

OFTEN FOUND

West End (Brisbane)

Redfern (Sydney)

Fitzroy (Melbourne)

The Bush

Anywhere that isn't of interest to mining
companies / urban developers

DISLIKES

Pauline Hanson

Coppers / Stereotypes

The First Australians are so-named because they are Indigenous to Australia, which means they were here first. They are also known as Blackfellas because they are black.

As a heavily politicised segment of the population, the First Australians are often put at the centre of national debate, despite representing only 2.5 per cent of the population and playing very little part in the day-to-day life of suburban Australia.

Because of this, First Australians are often tokenised and, while their cultural contributions to the Australian identity are celebrated with didgeridoos, sport and Aboriginal art, the community's very real social issues are often written off as whingeing, as in: 'These whingeing blacks are always putting their hands out for welfare,' or 'These whingeing blacks are always putting their hands out for a rational discussion on how to prevent the rise of diabetes and glaucoma in remote communities.'

While Paul Keating and Kevin Rudd have speeched themselves to the status of Great White Saviours, First Australians see little action from either side of politics when it comes to reparations or closing the gap in education and health.

Left-wing politics aims to intertwine hands singing 'Kumbaya' and spruik shallow promises of land rights, while right-wing politics focuses on asking questions like: 'You're only part Aboriginal though, aren't you?'

The First Australians have done more than impress in every single sport they've been involved in, and the same goes for arts. The greatest Australian painters are black and the greatest Australian rock bands are black, or at least they pretend they are (see: Midnight Oil).

The fact that the majority of First Australians live in regional communities has a range of disadvantages when it comes to living in contemporary Australia. For one, the health and education of young children is not often taken as seriously if those children live out the back of Bourke.

And two, blackfellas are often unable to transition to life among mainstream Australians without being asked weird questions about their experiences with discrimination, or if they can play the didgeridoo.

Their relationship with Hipsters (see: The Smashed Av) is a one-sided love affair. Meaning, they don't like Hipsters. Especially the ones who are moving into their inner-city hubs because it's so cheap and edgy.

THE BUSTED COCKY

OFTEN FOUND

The Bush

Mooloolaba on Australia Day

LIKES

The glory days of Australian football

Slim Dusty

Worcestershire Sauce

Cold meat on bread

DISLIKES

Being blamed for Indonesia's mistreatment of livestock

Being blamed for the bleaching of the Great Barrier Reef

Being blamed for the rise of One Nation

Coppers

The Busted Cocky is the Australian agriculturalist, which the rest of the population knows about, the drought-stricken, flood-stricken, tariff-stricken, Labor party punching bag.

While often held in high regard by political populists, they are mostly used for political point scoring in the same way war veterans are. 'What about our farmers?' is an expression that can be applied to almost every issue Pauline Hanson wants to apply it to.

Live export ban ... What about our farmers?
Foreign aid ... What about our farmers?
Halal-certification ... What about our farmers?
Inner-city crime wave involving at-risk Sudanese teenagers ... What about our farmers?

The Busted Cocky sits just behind the First Australian when it comes to being Australia's most-considered political minority. Whether they are clashing with each other, the media or with the government, both groups represent two separate, yet undeniably powerful, grassroots movements.

Despite their hostilities over what land belongs to who and why, even the most jaded Australian farmer will tell you they have more in common with the blackfellas than any professional politician in Canberra. Maybe it's their love of the bush, maybe it's the fact that if they don't make noise they'll get ignored, maybe it's because their kids always end up fucking off to the city and not visiting as much as they should.

The Busted Cocky represents that largest demographic of Australian farmers and is usually found in the most barren country with the harshest weather.

Unlike their agricultural enemy, the 'Bluebloods' – who tend to stick to their wheat and cotton farms in the Tuscan-like plains country – the Busted Cocky is working cattle and sheep, praying for rain and only getting to the beach house for two or three weeks over Christmas and Easter.

While they are often given the gesture of having a fellow Bushie as Deputy Prime Minister under a Coalition government, this doesn't stop the drought-ravaged farmer from feeling like their hard work feeding the country is being taken for granted. Especially when it takes 20 minutes to load *The Sydney Morning Herald* on their dial-up internet, only to be met with national headlines about whether Sydney University should implement genderless bathroom signs.

BET

COA

AUS

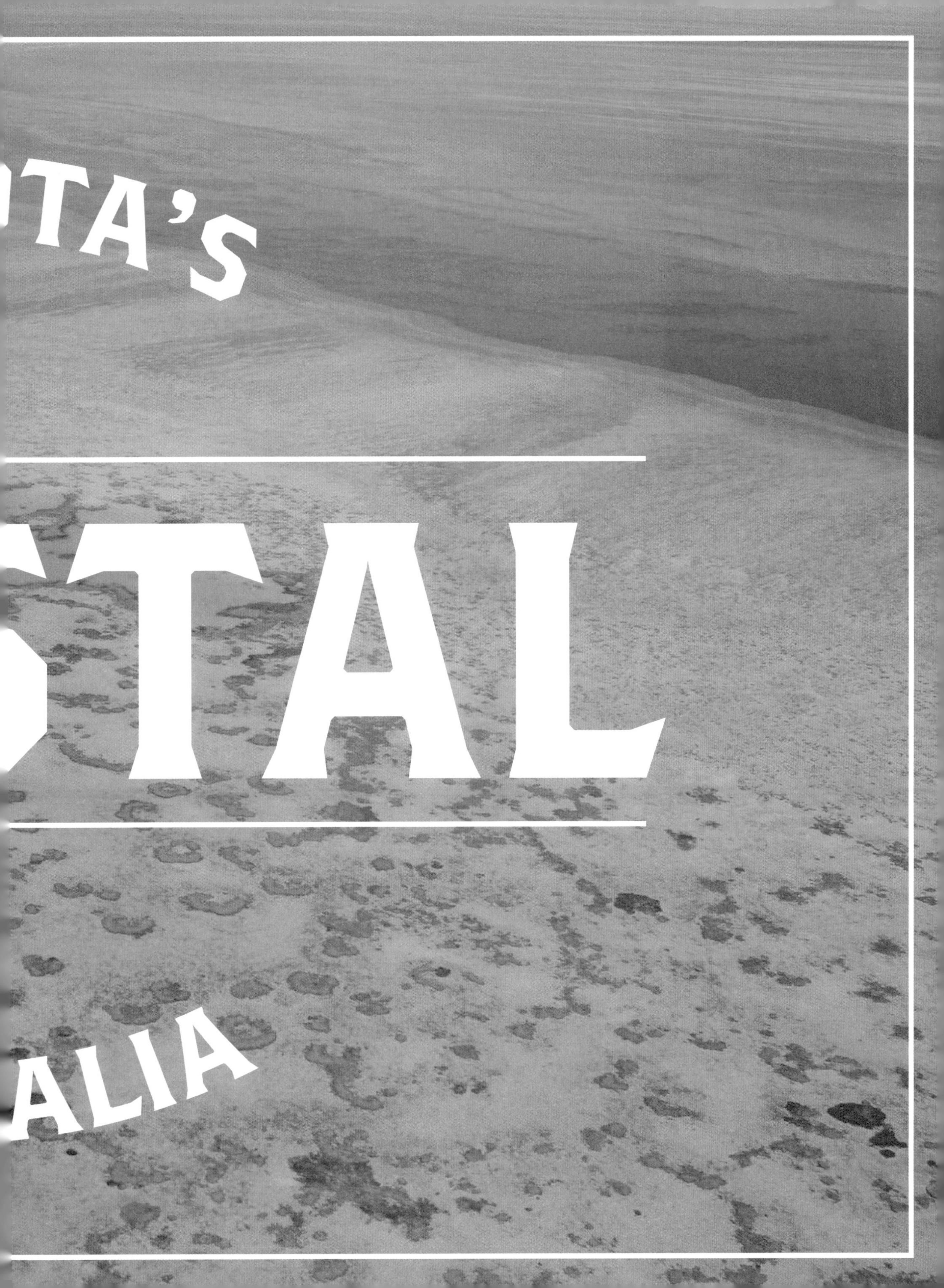
TA'S
STAL
ALIA

The BETOOTA ADVOCATE
NOW ONLINE!
VISIT
BETOOTAADVOCATE.COM

THE REGIONS

PLACES TO SEE

The Deep North

Central Coast & Newy

Adelaide

The West Coast

THE
DEEP NORTH

'It's just really good up here, ay [hahahah].' — Johnathan Thurston,
Cowboys Mad Monday, 2015

NOTABLE PEOPLE

Gorden Tallis (rugby league)

Julian Assange (WikiLeaks, WWIII)

Andrew Symonds (fishing, cricket)

Mitchell Johnson (cricket, moustache)

Eddie Mabo (the vibe)

THE DEEP NORTH

NOTABLE TOWNS

1. *Townsville*
2. *Cairns*
3. *Cooktown*
4. *Ingham*

Tourist hotspot Cairns, often pronounced as 'Cans' by locals.

Bordered by the Torres Strait Islands to the north, the Queensland Gulf Country to the west, the Great Barrier Reef to the east, and Central Queensland to the south, the Deep North is a rare patch of tropical Australia forged between an array of vastly different climatic regions.

Often likened to the USA's southern states, the Deep North is home to a diverse mix of cowboys, Pacific Islanders, blackfellas and, for some reason, Italians.

A naturally conservative population, with a natural hostility towards the Nation's southern empires, the Deep North has for many years called for secession. The basis being that Canberra, Sydney, Melbourne and even Brisbane are far too detached from their equatorial lifestyle.

The term of 'Southern Greed' is a common expression among the Northerners, who feel their natural resources and enterprise have been exploited by latte-sipping carpetbaggers since the beginning of Federation.

The historic trend of Sydney rugby league clubs stealing northern players with their big pokie-machine pay cheques has also been the cause of immense hostility, until the NRL decided to introduce the State of Origin competition. This meant each state could play the players they produced, without worrying about interstate money stealing their thunder. It is no secret that the Queensland Maroons would not have seen nearly as much success without the contributions of the Deep North.

While many Deep North rugby league purists have asked that the NRL take State of Origin football ☞

THE DEEP NORTH

LANDMARKS

1. Cairns

2. 1300 Smiles Stadium

3. Townsville

4. The Late Great Barrier Reef

5. Weipa

Below: The Great Barrier Reef, the world's largest living organism and a natural wonder of the world, unfortunately located right next to some really good coal.

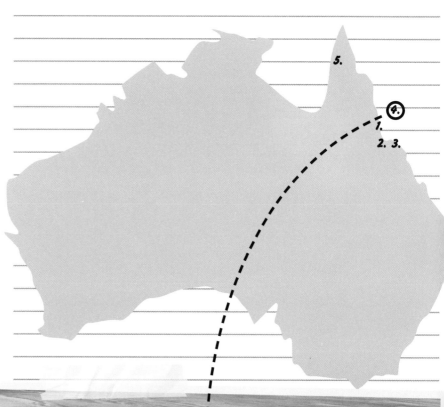

The still tropical waters of FNQ are often compared to Southern Florida. Just replace cocaine with dark spirits.

one step further by splitting the Maroons to create a third side, the Cowboys' 2015 club grand final win gave everyone enough proof that, even when paired up against Southern Queenslanders, the North will continue to rise.

The North Queensland Cowboys first played in the Australian Rugby League (ARL) premiership in 1995. In 1997 they broke away to join the rebel Super League competition, before playing in the reunified National Rugby League (NRL) competition the following year.

In 2015, the Cowboys played in the first all-Queensland grand final, defeating the Brisbane Broncos 17 to 16

DEBATES RAGE AS TO WHETHER THE NORTH QUEENSLAND COWBOYS PLAYERS ARE BETTER BEHAVED THAN THE SCANDAL-RIDDLED PLAYERS FROM DOWN SOUTH OR WHETHER THEY'RE JUST BETTER LOOKED AFTER.

in 'golden point' overtime to win their first, and to date only, premiership.

Based in the unofficial capital of the Deep North, Townsville, the Cowboys are the only professional sporting franchise within 1000 kilometres of their home ground, 1300 Smiles Stadium (formerly known as Dairy Farmers Stadium, despite the region not being very well known for dairy produce).

Their isolation means that, unlike the Southern footy franchises, the Cowboys are in a favourable position: all journalists, policeman, publicans and local residents support them.

Debates rage as to whether the North Queensland Cowboys players are better behaved than the scandal-riddled players from down south, or whether they're just better looked after by a town willing to waive petty

misdemeanours if it means they are going to win matches.

Fun fact: The only Cowboys player to ever experience a suspension as a result of off-field behaviour was a southern import, due to play for the NSW Origin side the following week. James Tamou learnt very quickly that blue isn't a good colour to be wearing when you get caught drunk behind the wheel.

CENTRAL COAST & NEWY

'It's better than Lego.' — Matty Johns, 1997

NOTABLE PEOPLE

Jennifer Hawkins (former Newcastle Knights cheerleader, former Miss Universe)

Nathan Tinkler (former Newcastle Knights owner, former billionaire)

Andrew Johns (former Newcastle Knights captain, 8th NRL Immortal)

Matty Johns (former Newcastle Knights Lego enthusiast, radio host)

Daniel Johns (former Newcastle Knights tee runner, Silverchair)

Jack Newton (former Newcastle Knights player's dad, pro-golfer)

Kasey Chambers (Country music singer-songwriter)

Belinda Clark (first Australian female cricketer to bat a double century)

Marcia Hines (former pop star)

Between Sydney's Northern Beaches and the vast national parks of Myall Lakes and Wallingat sits one of the oldest coastal regions in post-colonial Australia.

The Central Coast of NSW and its northern capital, Newcastle, has forever been home to the boat-builders, train-builders, steelworkers and coalminers that built this country.

While Newcastle is big enough and pretty enough to earn itself the census tag of 'metropolitan area', it is not close enough to Canberra or Sydney to keep their industries alive.

'Novocastrians' have for many years been kicking up a stink over the NSW state government's short-lived economic sugar hits that see train- and ship-building contracts sent to South-East Asian ☞

Terrigal Beach, home to some of the most famous ocean swells and political scandals in NSW.

CC & NEWY
NOTABLE TOWNS

1. Newcastle
2. Maitland
3. Raymond Terrace
4. The Entrance
5. Terrigal
6. Avoca Beach
7. Macmasters Beach
8. Gosford
9. Cessnock
10. Erina Fair

All other industries in the Central Coast/Hunter region pale in comparison to the sweet, sweet coal found near Newcastle.

manufacturers for a 5 per cent cheaper price and a 100 per cent less unionised workforce.

This has resulted in a tourism rebrand for the city, which was promptly followed by the ever-helpful state government implementing a Sydney-style alcohol curfew on live music venues and pubs.

However, aside from not featuring in nearly as many tourism ads as the Gold Coast or Tasmania, Newcastle has always had a lot to be proud of – namely, the perennial underdogs of the National Rugby League competition, the Newcastle Knights.

It is this footballing institution that has for many years forged a fierce loyalty between the city and its people. It is no lie that, even with the first signs of outsourcing and industrial decline, the 1990s was the greatest decade in Newcastle's long history culminating in a 1997 ARL Grand Final win. Residents of the Central Coast town of Newcastle had a lot to celebrate in the 1990s.

There was the development of the Stockton Bridge, which the town still holds close to its heart; there was the seemingly endless supply of high-paying blue-collar jobs on the wharfs, in the steel mill and in the factories building trains; and some of the greatest rock bands Australia has ever seen made their way out of the steel city and onto the airwaves of triple j.

Locals lament this lost decade of dominance in catch phrases.

'Steel, Silverchair and silverware' describes the abundance of jobs in steel milling, the greatest Australian band of the 1990s as well as the 'silverware' of several rugby league premierships.

Another common Novacastrian catch phrase is 'Sex, Drugs and Rock'n'Roll' used to describe Matty Johns, Andrew Johns and their distant cousin Daniel Johns respectively.

While anyone who is from Newcastle will proudly tell you, their Central Coast neighbours sit in purgatory between claiming Newy or Sydney.

Similarly to the long-suffering Deep North Queenslanders, residents of the great lakes are often overlooked by government and the media – with

CC & NEWY LANDMARKS

1. *Bluetongue Stadium, Gosford*
2. *Darby's Pie Bar, Newcastle*
3. *The Crown & Anchor Hotel, Newcastle*
4. *The Johns brothers household*
5. *Gosford Railway Station*
6. *Kincumber Macca's*
7. *Stockton Bridge, Newcastle*
8. *Fanny's Nightclub, Newcastle*

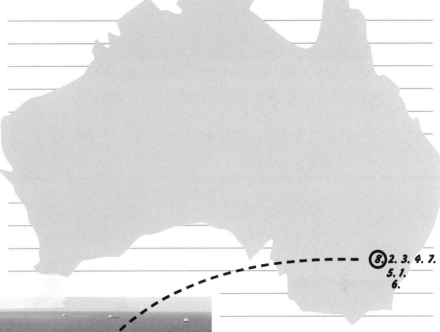

Newcastle, NSW. A town still high on the nineties.

other industry and infrastructure being awarded to their big-city neighbours.

The Central Coast has for many years been tipped as the next big thing in Australian tourism but, unluckily for them, Sydney's upper-echelon realised this well before their residents did.

This has resulted in very quiet winters for the beach towns of the 'Cenny Coast', while the investment bankers and lawyers from Down South leave their negatively geared beach houses vacant until it's warm enough for them to get their pale bodies out.

Recent technological advances have seen the beach towns of Macmasters, Avoca Beach and Terrigal become home to Australia's highest concentration of young dads playing with drones. So much so that the gentle buzz of these summer holidaymakers can even be heard from the lake capital of Gosford.

Aside from their economy being essentially dependent on whether or not Sydney wants to come to play for the weekend, Central Coast full-timers are well known for their fierce sense of community and local enterprise. Almost every resident is a member of a surf club, bowls club, football club or illegal motorcycle club.

Moona Moona Creek lagoon,
Huskisson, NSW

Port Douglas, Qld, Fran

Point Addis, Anglesea VIC –
Dana Grech

Brighton Beach, VIC –
Fran Gibson

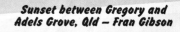

Sunset between Gregory and
Adels Grove, Qld – Fran Gibson

Stradbroke Island, Qld —
Fran Gibson

Low Isles, Great Barrier Reef,
Qld — Fran Gibson

Somewhere between Palm Cove
and Port Douglas — Luke Swan

ADELAIDE

'Did you know that we weren't settled by convicts?'
— Christopher Pyne, *Q&A*, 2014

NOTABLE PEOPLE

Shaun Micallef (ABC satirist/columnist)

Hilltop Hoods (Australia's Mobb Deep)

Trevor Chappell (greatest South Australian since Bradman)

Darren Lehmann (Australian cricketer)

John Aloisi (A-League journeyman)

David Hicks (former Australian ambassador to Cuba)

Alexander (Alick) Downer Sr (High Commissioner to England)

Sir Sidney Kidman (cattle baron)

The Superjesus (alt-rock troubadours)

Paul Kelly (singer/gravy magnate)

HG Nelson (sportswriter, panellist)

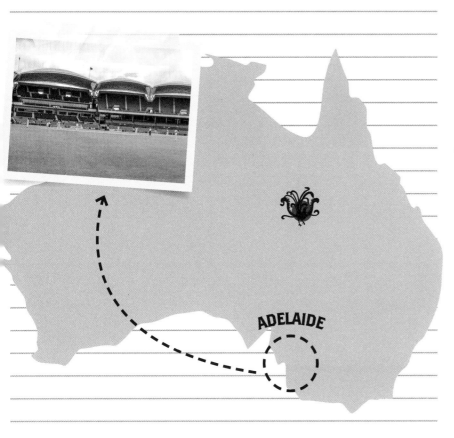

ADELAIDE LANDMARKS

Adelaide Oval
Christopher Pyne's shoe collection
Rundle Mall
The R.M. Williams factory
Victoria Square (Tarndanyangga)
River Torrens
Mega Adventure Park
The Gaol

Below: The Port of Adelaide, a body of water in South Australia's capital. Not to be confused with Port Adelaide, an AFL football team with racist fans.

Adelaide is our closest capital. There's not much you'll learn from the following that'll help you down there, but knowledge is power – especially when you're away from home.

Despite the proposal to shift to South Australian time being narrowly defeated in the 1998 local referendum, the people of Betoota still hold an affinity with what lesser capitals refer to as that 'Weird Place'. Though the national economy would only stand to benefit if it ceased to exist tomorrow, there are aspects of Adelaide that make it indispensable to the Australian identity.

The Torrens capital is home to one of Australia's lowest rates of petty theft. Only 1 per cent of residents admitted to stealing a Mars Bar from a newsagency in their youth. That's compared to the national ☞

average of 94 per cent – a stunning inverse statistic. You're also 40 times less likely to have your car keyed for parking like a prick.

This is down to the fact that Adelaide, as you've been told a thousand times before, was a free settlement – meaning there were no convicts allowed. Science has proven, more than once, that nearly all petty and non-violent crime in Australia is committed by people with convict blood running through their veins. Wearing a wallet chain in Adelaide is not necessary.

After a big night out, it's not unknown for people around town to make the drive down the Adelaide Road to Port Augusta for some McDonald's. Some swear that while the Roma one may be a little bit further, the road is better. That's up to you to decide.

Nevertheless, for all that Adelaide

ADELAIDE, AS YOU'VE BEEN TOLD A THOUSAND TIMES BEFORE, WAS A FREE SETTLEMENT – MEANING THERE WERE NO CONVICTS ALLOWED.

and Betoota have in common, there's a reason why we live in Queensland.

If you walk into any pub in Adelaide expecting a few cheap schoons, with the rugby league playing softly in the background, you'll leave disappointed. The only thing rarer than petty crime

in Adelaide is a cheap beer; be sure to fill up a hip flask with rum and spend the evening sorting yourself out with schmiddies of cola.

The extremely low crime rate and popular nightlife really do make it a pleasure to visit, even for the

The City of Churches, Adelaide has been desperately trying to rebrand since the Royal Commission.

Left & right: The artistic and cultural precinct of Rundle Mall, a nightlife and live music destination since Sydney's lock-out laws.

most bush-drunk youngster from the Channels. It is only here that a young Betootan can really cut his teeth in the big old city, before heading to somewhere more advanced like Mooloolaba or Noosa.

So if you're looking for a place to go and ease yourself into a town that doesn't sleep, visit Adelaide. It's the training wheels a desert youth needs, before you head to a city with one-punch laws and hip-hop music. In the words of the mayor, sit back and relax. Let the good times roll.

THE
WEST COAST

'I thought the Greeks were lying about the money to be made in Australia. That was until I saw how shit you skippies were at farming pearls.' — Nicholas Paspaley Senior, MBE

NOTABLE PEOPLE

Kim Beazley (former Deputy Prime Minister)

Tim Winton (author)

Heath Ledger (actor)

Jim Jefferies (comedian)

Lisa McCune (actor)

Elizabeth Durack (artist and writer)

Farris Brothers (founders of rock band INXS)

Lang Hancock (mining magnate)

Gina Rinehart (daughter of Lang)

Tame Impala (rock band)

Ernie Dingo ('Getaway')

Believe it or not, there's a place more isolated than Betoota. And it's not Perth. The honour goes to Kiwirrkurra, a small community in Western Australia in the Gibson Desert. Port Hedland lies 1200 km to the west and Alice Springs 850 km to the east.

However, the West Coast is quite isolated in general.

While the population of Kiwirrkurra stands at about a quarter of Betoota's, the total population of Western Australia is more than 2 million – meaning close to 10 per cent of the entire country lives in almost abject isolation, cut off from that which even Betootanese folk would consider cosmopolitan.

Even so, that hasn't prevented the true island state from contributing to the nation's bottom line, time and time again. ☞

The quokka is an unofficial official mascot for Western Australia, alongside the Swan and West ~~Coke~~ Coast Eagle.

WEST COAST LANDMARKS

1. BankWest Tower
2. Central Park Tower
3. Fremantle Prison
4. The Old Mill
5. Lincoln Street ventilation stack
6. Bunbury Lighthouse
7. Rottnest Island
8. Dirk Hartog's pewter dish
9. WACA Ground
10. Margaret River

Despite what Bernard Fanning suggests, Western Australia is actually the only place you will see a sunset over the beaches.

Upon your arrival in Perth, please take the time to thank each person you encounter for their selfless GST donations over the years, and explain that a number of public infrastructure projects and improvements to budget bottom lines wouldn't have been possible without the sacrifices made by the people of the West.

If the people of Australia didn't have the West, we'd be a lesser nation. Explain that point to them, too.

Betoota has a lot in common with the West Coast.

First, owing to the West's isolation, there are a wide variety of competitive sporting competitions. The South African and Zimbabwean immigrants were pivotal in introducing and maintaining a number of cricket and rugby union clubs – although League has yet to take off. Victorian Rules is also remarkably popular on the West Coast, which is able to support two representative sides.

Also, like the Betootanese, people in the West have a unique accent. Not dissimilar to the Melbourne or Free Settler accents, it is unique enough to justify its own subcategory: the Perth Accent (see page 184, Language section).

However, that's where a lot of similarities end.

IF THE PEOPLE OF AUSTRALIA DIDN'T HAVE THE WEST, WE'D BE A LESSER NATION.

The Betootanese music scene is incomparable to that of the West Coast. As a youth, you may have been familiar with the Perth and Fremantle music scene – or you may not have been. Acts such as Tame Impala, AC/DC, San Cisco and Jebediah (and all other Kevin Parker–related projects) have become popular around the world. Whereas the greatest musical talent to come out of our great district is John Forgert, who learnt how to play 'Brown Eyed Girl' for his brother's wedding in 1998.

One last thing to remember when visiting the West Coast: it's not just Perth and Fremantle. There are many great places to see up and down the coast, from Margaret River to Shark Bay. But like the Gulf Country, try to keep out of the water because you might – and probably will – be eaten by a shark.

TRY TO KEEP OUT OF THE WATER BECAUSE YOU MIGHT – AND PROBABLY WILL – BE EATEN BY A SHARK.

Come have a dip

Betoota Sailing Club

194 Birdsville Developmental Road, Betoota

THE LOCALS

NOTABLE TYPES

The Jet-Ski Owner

People Who Say 'Yeeew'

The QueeNZlander

The Boomer

THE
JET-SKI OWNER

OFTEN FOUND

Carindale/Mount Gravatt (Brisbane)

Hills District (Sydney)

Sylvania Waters (Sutherland Shire, Sydney)

Western Australia (in general)

Cairns (Qld)

Gold Coast (Qld)

Werribee (Melbourne)

Adelaide Plains (SA)

Canberra (ACT)

ALSO KNOWN AS

Crown Lager's target demographic

Cubbies, CUBs (cashed-up bogans)

LIKES

Lucrative jobs in the mines

Kuta Beach

Air con

Home cinemas

Motorsports

DISLIKES

Political correctness

Politicians

Coppers

The cost of fuel

Whatever Mark Latham dislikes

The Jet-Ski Owner (JSO) is a term given to the Australian nouveau riche, or 'new money', which makes up one of Australia's largest suburban demographics.

With young families as well as boats in tow, their name comes from this subculture's love of impulse purchases and alcohol-fuelled water sports.

Although a relatively new social class, the JSO came into being after the WA and Queensland mining booms saw a large portion of Australia's working class rise from the swamps of fibro shacks to the dizzy heights of rendered-brick McMansions.

It was from here that they forged a new culture of material status.

Often employed as non-unionised blue-collar employees in predominantly white industries that aren't threatened by foreign manufacturing, the Jet-Ski Owner is known for its unique political sentiments, which are successfully targeted by populist minor political parties each election.

The JSO's main issue with contemporary Australian politics is the fact that no one is addressing the real issues, like the ever-increasing cost of living for middle-class Australians who own two four-wheel drives, a

jet ski and a giant rendered-brick house in the suburbs. They put this detachment down to politicians being too focused on minorities and the environment, as well as lining their own pockets.

Following a steep decline in mining jobs, the JSO is now resorting to making money in retail – after discovering how cheap it is to get shit made in China – and oil and gas FIFO work (fly in/fly out).

To the JSO, climate scientists and environmentalists are as full of shit as those pussy sports doctors, who keep complaining about the dangers of concussion in football.

PEOPLE
WHO SAY 'YEEEW'

OFTEN FOUND	ALSO KNOWN AS	LIKES
Sunshine Coast (Qld)	Surfies	Surfing
Gold Coast (Qld)	Dune Rats	Fishing
Fremantle (WA)	The Boys	Skating
Mornington Peninsula (Vic)		Rock music
Coffs Harbour (NSW)	**DISLIKES**	Road trips
Newcastle (NSW)		Weird coastal towns
Central Coast (NSW)	Blow-ins & Drop-ins	Oporto's
Northern Beaches (NSW)	Flat spells	Surf checks
Wollongong (NSW)	SUP's	Shoeys
	Razor scooters	

From the early days of Australian surfing and skating, the sun-kissed Aussies who rose to the top were world-renowned for their good looks, mysterious demeanour and fashion sense. However, the cheeky-joint and panel-van subculture slowly became the norm for all young people in beach towns. The days of Michael Peterson and Mark Occhilupo are now behind us.

No longer is this community limited to the handsome school dropouts who could ride waves. It now encompasses all walks of life, including some who don't even live near the beach.

After a brief 'bad boy phase' in the late '90s, this scene has also outgrown the Bra Boys (Maroubra) and Palmy Army (Palm Beach) punch-on brand of water-based youth culture. It's now become a vast community centred around the love of surfing, skating, fishing and music.

The term 'yeeew' is a catchcry of skateboarders and surfies, used to highlight something that is fucking sick – often relating to surf conditions, extreme outdoor activities, binge drinking and the relatively new phenomenon of binge marijuana use.

While not entirely free of the tribal, headland-to-headland hostilities usually associated with a culture that many individuals feel should be limited to 'locals only' – Australia's longhaired louts are now known for their relatively chilled out attitude towards everything except partying.

That, and surfing, skating and fishing. The rise of Aussie rock groups Dune Rats and Violent Soho helped solidify this relaxed culture who, up until the release of 'Covered In Chrome', had felt their lifestyle was only represented by The Mad Hueys iconic surfing and fishing videos.

One fatal flaw that the Yeeew community face is the toxic momentum of one-upmanship. Constantly chasing bigger thrills to break out of the cannabis slumber can result in a brand of mob mentality that is known to hurt and kill.

Watching one of your mates jump off a pelting CountryLink train and land in a questionably low river below is never enough … and the fact that it can be done without injury only makes it an instant right of passage for 'the boys'.

Smoking 32 cones in one sitting, just because your mate did 31 last week, isn't necessarily something people do for fun – and will probably lead to hours spent vomiting on oneself in the ceramic base of a beach shack shower.

Much like other male-centric subcultures, the hysteria of being a young Australian male can only be soothed by strong, argumentative girlfriends, and sisters who know a fucking try-hard when they see one.

THE QUEENZLANDER

OFTEN FOUND

Logan (Qld)

Gold Coast (Qld)

Cairns (Qld)

Mackay (Qld)

Townsville (Qld)

Inala (Qld)

Ipswich (Qld)

Dee Why (NSW)

ALSO KNOWN AS

FOBs / Kiwis / Sole

Dox / Uce / Toko

LIKES

Scaffolding

Having a feed

The All Blacks

Queensland Maroons

DISLIKES

The Wallabies

NSW Blues

Other people of Polynesian background whose families don't come from the same specific Island nation as theirs

Coppers

Despite the relatively offensive nickname, no other people of colour have been welcomed into Australian culture as warmly and smoothly as the FOB (Fresh Off Boat).

Their undeniable contribution to Australia's rugby codes, pub safety and the temporary steel structures on construction sites has resulted in a close and important relationship with working-class Australia.

Many of the older QueeNZlanders have, in their lifetime, lived in both the sunny Pacific islands, the cold and rainy islands of New Zealand, and eventually the dry and humid suburbs of Australia.

Because their tropical roots of Samoa, Fiji, Tonga and the Cook Islands share a similar climate to Australia's northern towns, most FOBs hold Queensland close to their heart – even the poor buggers who ended up in the chilly Southern states.

While Maoris are also often closely associated with FOB communities, their place in Australia dates back to colonial eras, whereas QueeNZlanders only came into the public eye when the Kefu brothers and Lote Tuqiri made their mark on Super Rugby and NRL respectively.

Before the influx of Polynesian talent to Australian sport, the most famous FOB in Australia was the TV entertainer 'Vulcan' from Gladiators.

In fact, FOBs have become so integral to Australian culture that the only notable throwback to their Pacific Island backgrounds is their undying intergenerational love for the New Zealand All Blacks. Even the boys and girls who end up playing for Australian rugby teams are known to keep a pair of black footy shorts in their sports bags.

An interesting cultural phenomenon, which has resulted from close ties between Polynesian Australians and working-class whites, is the 'bro-ing' of teenage white kids.

Adopting a Kiwi-style Mohawk mullet and fake Polynesian accent is common for young white men who are exposed to the strong community, dance, music and culture of FOB-Australians through school and sport.

Many of our Polynesian brothers are devout, church-going Christians – but it's the Northern Queensland FOBs who are better known for their manners and conservative haircuts. South-east corner FOBs are more likely to get a bit of non-tribal ink and take Dad's Tarago for an underage spin.

It's because of this that the term 'F-Plates' has entered the Australian vernacular, as a way of describing unlicensed driving.

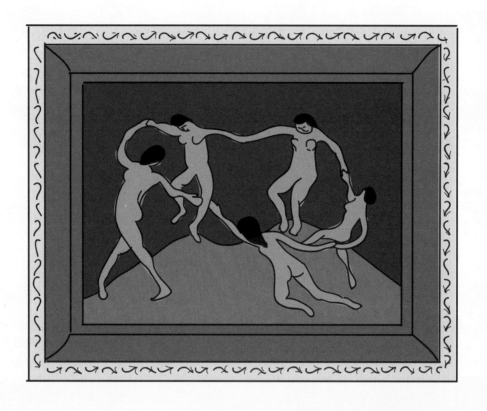

THE
BOOMER

OFTEN FOUND

Racecourse Road (Brisbane)

North Shore Sydney

Inner West Sydney

Cottesloe Beach (Perth)

Byron Bay (Northern Rivers, NSW)

Noosa (Sunshine Coast, Qld)

Toorak (Melbourne)

Adelaide Hills

ALSO KNOWN AS

Baby Boomers

Generation I (Never Had It Easy)

Whitlam's Problem Children

LIKES

Questioning modern parenting techniques

Not paying for university degrees

Owning several properties

Gentrification

DISLIKES

Going to war

Noisy pubs

Retiring

Whatever Andrew Bolt dislikes

O nce upon a time, there was a clear and concise moment in someone's professional life that suggested it was maybe time to pack it in. However, with modern medicine and the ability to have ever-relevant opinions through social media, 60 has become the new 40.

Enter the Boomer. Despite a disastrous track record – fiddling with the environment, declaring wars they forget about and warehousing scallywags inside prisons – our great nation is still being run by people born during the post World War II baby boom (1946–64).

Initially known for their flower-powered enthusiasm for LSD in the late 60s, this particular generation – known as the 'Baby Boomers' – have been heavily criticised over the last 30 years for their radical transition from humanitarians to self-serving wealth hoarders.

Many refuse to leave their high-powered positions in the corporate sector, or free up the crowded housing market by retiring to the coast or country, as was the template they created for their own parents.

In Australia, more and more of our cities have been forced to close all live music venues at midnight.

This is due to the fact that the majority of state governments and police forces are dictated to by Boomers, who have grown sick of inner-city noise levels disrupting them while they're trying to watch re-runs of small-town BBC murder mysteries.

While climate change is a very real issue for Generation Y and Generation X, the Boomers are focusing their attention on culling sharks and criticising younger generations for not having enough elbow grease to fix these problems, which couldn't have been avoided, no matter what scientists say.

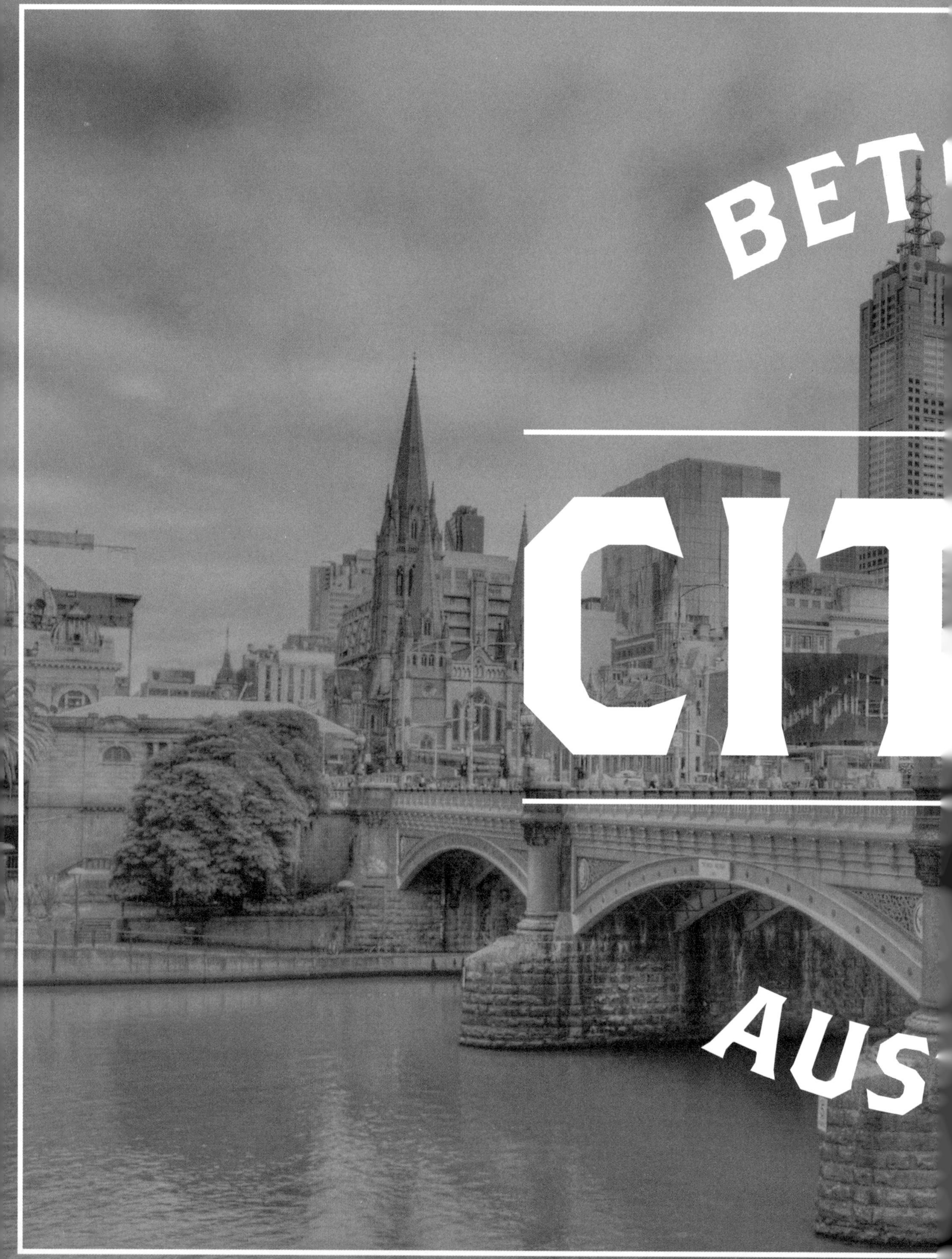
BET
CIT
AUS

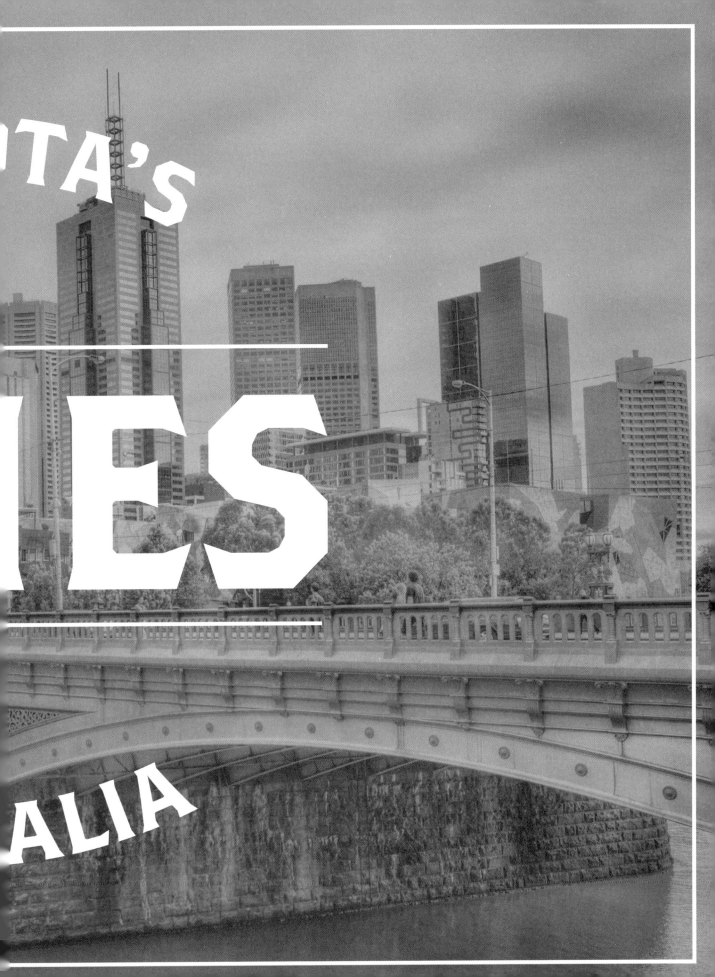

Betoota Polo Association

Inconvenient locations | Uncomfortable dress codes | Useless networking
The people are just like you!

THE BIG SMOKES

PLACES TO SEE

South-East Corner

Sydney

Canberra

Melbourne

SOUTH-EAST
CORNER, QLD

'We were the dirty, ugly cousins for quite a few years. If Brisbane was seated at a wedding we wouldn't get the seats up the front, we'd be at the back with the cousins that you don't want to talk to.' – Katie Noonan, 2016.

NOTABLE PEOPLE

Steven 'The Pearl' Renouf (rugby league)

Kay McGrath (Channel 7 News)

Sarina Russo (Sarina Russo)

Bernard Fanning (Powderfinger)

Karl Stefanovic (breakfast TV)

Margaret Olley (artist)

Stefan Ackerie (shampoo magnate)

Stephanie Rice (Olympian)

John Eales (rugby union)

Darren Hayes (Savage Garden)

Wally Lewis (Qld royal family)

Anna Bligh (former Qld premier, Australian Bankers' Association)

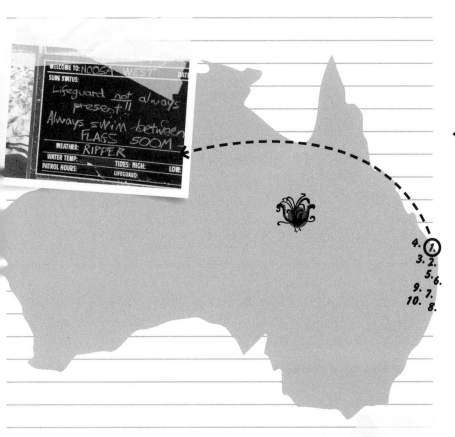

SOUTH-EAST CORNER

NOTABLE TOWNS

1. Noosa
2. Mooloolaba
3. Kingaroy
4. Gympie
5. Caboolture
6. Redcliffe
7. Brisbane
8. Gold Coast
9. Ipswich
10. Logan City

WELCOME TO: NOOSA WEST
SURF STATUS:
Lifeguard not always present!!
Always swim between FLAGS 500M
WEATHER: RIPPER
WATER TEMP:
PATROL HOURS: TIDES: HIGH: LOW:
LIFEGUARD:

South Bank Beach, 'The Ganges of the South'.

The great South-East Queensland (SEQ) is the biggest and most populated bio-geographical, political and administrative region in Australia.

Stretching from the retirement hub of Hervey Bay to the New South Wales border, the Queensland capital of Brisbane has morphed into quite the megatropolis over the last two decades.

While its people are known for their lighter brand of Queensland conservatism and their basic open-mindedness to the perversion and sin that has become normalised in the Southern states, the 'Big Country Town' tag is not leaving the South-East anytime soon – no matter how many high-rise apartments they build.

Centred on the spiritual Brisbane River estuary, known as the 'Brown ☞

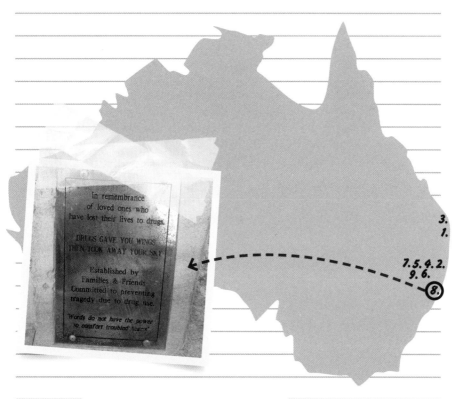

Snake', the South-East Corner runs along the only strip of Queensland coastline that actually has waves. However, politicians are confident that, if the coral bleaching of the Great Barrier Reef keeps up, Northern Queensland towns will soon be able to market themselves as 'surf getaways' as well.

The dress code of the South-East is as unique as their politicians' last names (Bjelke-Petersen, Soorley, Pisasale, Palaszczuk), with fusions of the bush, kiwi culture and loud colours.

For women, bright-patterned dresses and jumpsuits with large showings of gold and silver jewellery is a common look for the nightlife destinations of Sunshine Coast, Brisbane and Cavill Avenue. The 'beehive' haircut is often synonymous with the 'ghetto fab' SEQ female.

Men's clothing is a lot less experimental, with the 'concrete cowboy' model being completely acceptable in the eyes of most nightclub bouncers. This formula

SOUTH-EAST CORNER

LANDMARKS

1. The Surf Club, Mooloolaba

2. The 'Brown Snake', Brisbane

3. 'Palmersaurus',
Clive Palmer's dinosaur park, Coolum Beach

4. Lang Park, Brisbane

5. Stefan's Skyneedle, Brisbane

6. South Logan Rugby League Club

7. Sunnybank Plaza, Brisbane

8. The 'Glitter Strip',
Cavill Avenue, Surfers Paradise

9. Arthur Gorrie Correctional Centre, Wacol

After nearly 200 years on the banks of a tidal river, Brisbane is not yet familiar with, or prepared for, the concept of floods.

The quintessential Byron Bay resident. Most often wealthy expatriated city youth whose parents think they are studying.

usually includes R.M. Williams shoes, checked shirts, chino trousers and a haircut that sits above the ears.

So common is the leather dress boot in SEQ, for both men and women, that it has almost become compulsory in different venues around Brisbane.

Another region often associated with the South-East Corner is the Northern Rivers capital Byron Bay. While located just south of the NSW border, the area is often viewed as an extension of the megatropolis.

Byron Bay, while actually home to generations of actual residents, has in recent years become a hub for a transient community of underachieving expatriated Queensland and Sydney city youths. These make up 60 per cent of the population and form the basis for Byron and Lennox Head's new nickname: 'far north Bondi'.

Hysterical property markets have seen many young ex-private schoolers relocating from their family Queenslander homes to the beach town, where they immerse themselves in the faux-hippy lifestyle and a damaging sense of entitlement.

Brisbane city is well known for inheriting the occasional hemp linen shirt and train-driver hat, worn by 'Byron locals' who are returning home from their post-war beach shack that they share with six other people, while working on an online commerce platform for Balinese-made jewellery and sarongs, to ask Mum and Dad for a bit of help with the bills.

The South-East Corner is also known as a breeding ground for some

MEN'S CLOTHING... USUALLY INCLUDES R.M. WILLIAMS SHOES, CHECKED SHIRTS, CHINO TROUSERS AND A HAIRCUT THAT SITS ABOVE THE EARS.

of Australia's greatest footballers from all codes – including the Victorian game.

It is because of this that the residents have had to make a conscious effort to find celebrities not associated with sport. This

has resulted in some very obscure household names, such as Stefan Ackerie (shampoo celebrity), Sarina Russo (recruitment celebrity), Tim 'Sharky' Ward (Gold Coast crime figure) and Tuffy (bloke who plays live cover music at a few pubs).

Surfers Paradise, Qld — Fran Gibson

Leichhardt Oval — Bryce T.

Darwin — Andrew Permezel

Flemington cricket club on Wo
Ascot Vale in Melbourne — Toa

Surfers Paradise, Qld —
Fran Gibson

Surfers Paradise, Qld

In remembrance
of loved ones who
have lost their lives to drugs.

DRUGS GAVE YOU WINGS
THEN TOOK AWAY YOUR SKY

Established by
Families & Friends
Committed to preventing
tragedy due to drug use.

"Words do not have the power
to comfort troubled hearts"

Allianz Stadium — @thejimclasshero

SYDNEY

'To peer deeply into this ghost city, the one lying beneath the surface, is to understand that Sydney has a soul and that it is a very dark place indeed.' — John Birmingham, *Leviathan*, 1999

NOTABLE PEOPLE

Malcolm Turnbull (Prime Minister, Goldman Sachs)

Mike Baird (former NSW premier, NAB)

Nicole Kidman ('Eyes Wide Shut')

Mario Fenech (rugby league)

Jeff Fenech (boxing)

Roxy Jacenko (Sweaty Betty PR)

Russell Crowe (rugby league, Gladiator)

Ian Thorpe (Olympian)

Deng Adut (The Betoota Advocate's lawyer)

Anthony Mundine (boxing, rugby league)

Missy Higgins (folk-rock singer, property investor)

Once known as the most exciting, bizarre, dangerous and sexed-up city in the world, Sydney, NSW, has come a long way in recent years.

Much like how the rowdy colonial empires of Singapore and Hong Kong were able to – with capital punishment – reclaim their cities from the transient and colourful characters who roamed their streets, Sydney has been able to do it with tolls, roadwork and property prices.

It appears that their often-teased sense of Southern self-importance has paid off, with thousands of people around Australia and the world convincing themselves that Sydney is where they need to live.

Aside from centuries of state government corruption, appalling town planning and an unaffordable cost of living, Sydney's beaches are ☞

The Bondi rockpool. It is advised that one does not go swimming while under the influence of Bondi Marching Powder.

SYDNEY
NOTABLE TOWNS

SYDNEY

Balmain
Kirribilli
Mosman
Manly
Bondi
Lakemba
Parramatta
Penrith
Maroubra
Redfern
Newtown
Cabramatta
Cronulla

The Sydney Harbour Bridge, also known as 'The Coathanger'.

enough of a counterargument to justify visiting there.

Anyone will tell you that the sprawling sands and boomerang coves of Manly, Bondi, Maroubra and Cronulla are some of the best in the world, and the ocean walks along the Pacific-facing headlands are loved by all, except by the gay men who kept getting thrown off them by policemen and youth gangs in the '80s.

However, while still aesthetically pleasing, the city's unique bohemian spark is fading. Gone are the days of Brett Whiteley and Jimmy Barnes eating their breakfast at Sweethearts – the city is now looking to sterilise its streets and further blow air into an ever-expanding property bubble that analysts cannot predict, understand or stop.

The city has restricted the retail

THE ONCE DODGY AND WILD STREETS OF SYDNEY NOW LOOK LIKE POST-DIG POMPEII.

SYDNEY LANDMARKS

Sydney Opera House
Sydney Harbour Bridge
Bondi Beach
Redfern Convenience Store
The Star Casino
Barangaroo
Rooty Hill RSL

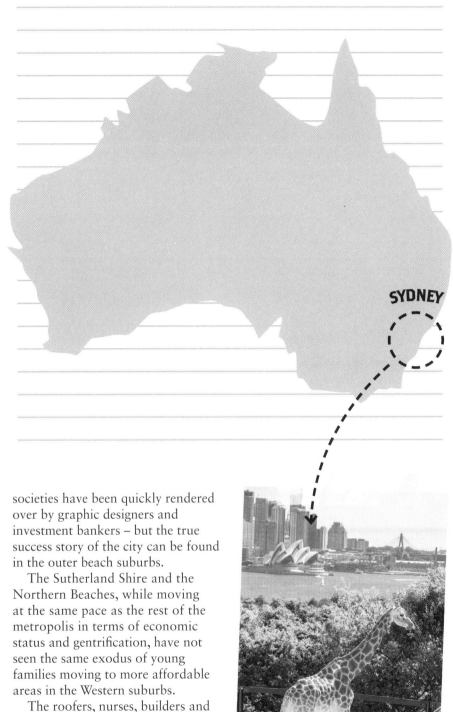

hours of music venues and Turkish fast food outlets, and all public transport services end before midnight. The once dodgy and wild streets of Sydney now look like post-dig Pompeii.

The glamorous drag queens who once glided down the pavements of Oxford Street have been replaced by parking inspectors and Deliveroo cyclists, as the city's remaining youth cut their losses and download TV-streaming services to fill the King Cross–sized hole in their young adulthood.

In the last two decades, Australians from across the nation have made their way to the Harbour and Eastern Suburbs for a taste of the fledgling community of working-class Sydney. But now, the once-proud wharfie suburb of Balmain is nothing more than off-site accommodation for the senior ranks of the ABC.

The city's Post-war Wogs have capitalised hard on any remaining grunge found in their inner-west enclaves. Who knew owning a bike shop could make you a millionaire, if you put a teenager in there with a coffee maker?

The unity and tensions of one of Australia's first true multicultural societies have been quickly rendered over by graphic designers and investment bankers – but the true success story of the city can be found in the outer beach suburbs.

The Sutherland Shire and the Northern Beaches, while moving at the same pace as the rest of the metropolis in terms of economic status and gentrification, have not seen the same exodus of young families moving to more affordable areas in the Western suburbs.

The roofers, nurses, builders and shopkeepers of these tough rugby league coastal hubs have stayed, risen with the swamp and built their own waterfront mansions. The Jet-Ski Owners, as they are now known, have proven that when you are on to a good thing, you don't always need to sell up.

Taronga Zoo, Sydney. The last bastion of undeveloped waterfront harbour real estate.

CANBERRA

'I have planned a city not like any other city in the world. I have planned it not in a way that I expected any governmental authorities in the world would accept' — Walter Burley Griffin, 1912, *The New York Times*

NOTABLE PEOPLE

Mick Molloy (comedian, AFL commentator)

James Hird (former Victorian Football player/coach, alternative medicine activist)

Patty Mills (NBA player)

Sam Norton-Knight (former rugby union player)

Lee Efrossynis

CANBERRA
LANDMARKS

The Australian War Memorial
Questacon
Some art galleries
High Court of Australia
Captain Cook Memorial Jet
Scrivener Dam
The Telstra Tower
Mooseheads Pub & Nightclub
Most of Yarralumla
Lake Burley Griffin

Top right: Canberra, ACT. Also known as 'The Bush Capital'.
Bottom: Australian Parliament House, also known as 'The Trough'.

Canberra is a tale of two cities but, unlike Dickens' *A Tale of Two Cities*, it doesn't explore the possibilities of resurrection and transformation on a personal and a societal level.

Parliament and government is the appendix of the large intestine that is the Great Bush Capital. When, or if, you even find yourself there, exercise the same rule that you would when visiting a dangerous capital city: never stray further than a kilometre from a major body of water.

However, in Canberra, that means keeping an eye on Lake Burley Griffin at all times. Or to be within a quick run of it at least.

Our Federal Member in Canberra, the Hon. David Littleproud, has agreed to lend you the parliamentary ☞

Glock 23 if you need to attend to business in Canberra further than a kilometre from the Lake. Note each round you use has to be recorded, so no shooting road signs – no matter how great the temptation is. David can also pick you up at the airport if he's got the time. His phone number is on page 203. But don't ask if you can stay at his place; he already sleeps on Bob Katter's floor.

Aside from the danger that lurks in the more perilous parts of Canberra, such as Tuggeranong, Red Hill and Fyshwick, the capital is a pleasant place to visit. This guide recommends that seeing Canberra should be high on your to-do list. It also makes for a pleasant stopover between Sydney and Melbourne, if you sufficiently hate yourself enough to drive the length of the Hume Highway.

Canberra can offer you something

IT ALSO MAKES FOR A PLEASANT STOPOVER BETWEEN SYDNEY AND MELBOURNE IF YOU SUFFICIENTLY HATE YOURSELF ENOUGH TO DRIVE THE LENGTH OF THE HUME HIGHWAY.

Top/Bottom: Canberra is home to some of Australia's most iconic memorials, galleries and public art sculptures.

other cities simply cannot. As a glorified country town, its sense of community isn't too far removed from other parts of regional Australia. Just last year, the international airport terminal opened, offering direct flights to Singapore and Wellington ... only a year after Emirates began offering direct flights from Remienko International Airport in South Betoota to Kabul. Canberra is a town on the move.

The skinny of this is: visiting the capital is something you should do at least once, but be careful and keep close to the Lake. Make sure not to carry large amounts of cash and try to keep your valuables hidden in public. Canberra is a dog-eat-dog town.

MELBOURNE

'A large provincial English city paradoxically in far south-east Asia.'
— Barry Humphries, 2015

NOTABLE PEOPLE

Barry Humphries (actor, comedian)

Graham Kennedy (entertainer)

Kylie Minogue (pop princess)

360 (hip-hop artist)

Tina Arena (pop singer)

Eric Bana (actor)

Sir Edward 'Weary' Dunlop

Flea (bassist for Red Hot Chilli Peppers)

Hemsworth et al.

The other Alan Jones

Keith Miller (former Test cricketer)

Rupert Murdoch

The people you encounter in Melbourne rarely consider themselves Australians. They consider themselves to be above Australians – which they probably are.

In the Gold Rush years, between 1850 and 1870, Melbourne was the richest city on the planet. Some of the greatest examples of Victorian architecture are still present in the city.

Some even claim that the Victorian movement began in Melbourne. There is little evidence to prove otherwise. St Kilda Road was once deemed to be one of the great avenues on Earth – together with the Champs-Élysées in Paris and Oxford Street in London.

However, for all their cultural currency and morality, a number of historical events happened in Melbourne that one should know about before forming an opinion on the place.

Melbourne was founded by a group of people from Launceston, in the Democratic Peoples' Republic of Tasmania, who arrived in 1836. They made a deal with eight Wurundjeri elders for the land and the city was born. However, it was originally named Batmania, after founder John Batman. Interesting.

The Yarra Capital is also where the White Australia Policy was first put into practice. Towards the end of the gold rush, swathes of boats laden with mostly Chinese migrants were turned away from Port Phillip Bay. Like with most things, Melbourne was doing it before it was popular.

But for all the disservice Melbourne has done to the nation, Victorians have contributed in their own unique way – through the language of sport.

Victorian Rules Football, or Australian Rules as it's known in Melbourne, is one of the state's greatest exports. The game is played in a handful of nations around the world. There is even some suggestion that it's almost as popular as cricket in some parts of the United States and Canada. A marvellous feat for a game that was allegedly invented by the First Australians who, as legend would have it, would kick around a possum hide full of gum leaves.

Only a small number of Betootanese people have been to the Victorian capital and returned to speak of what they saw. Should you find yourself down there, please make sure to write to us about your experiences. It would be a great ☞

Aside from graffitied laneways, Melbourne struggles to differentiate itself from Sydney. Lucky they have coffee.

MELBOURNE

MELBOURNE LANDMARKS

Hume Highway

Lane of Graffiti

Café inside Lane

Federation Square

Electric buses on tracks

Melbourne Cricket Ground

Crown Casino

Culture

The Princes Bridge, a perfect example of Victoria's Victorian style of Victorian-era architecture and the oldest river crossing in Australia.

IT'S HEAVILY FROWNED UPON TO RUN OVER CYCLISTS.

service to not only Betoota but the wider Diamantina community.

It's also recommended to bring instant coffee with you, as finding it in Melbourne is nigh on impossible. Only a small black market exists, serving mainly the Queensland expat community.

One thing to remember is that, if you find yourself in trouble, you can visit Cenzo Devine's brother-in-law at his Italian restaurant in Carlton. He's agreed to help out any young Betootanese resident if they are lost or injured.

Also, be sure to listen carefully to how Melbournians speak. They're speaking English but the dialect is sometimes difficult for native Betootanese Pidgin speakers to decipher. If you speak Interior English as a second language, then the task becomes easier.

Two things to remember when driving in Melbourne: you turn left from the right lane and Greens voters always have right of way. Also, it's heavily frowned upon to run over cyclists. It is recommended you don't do that.

Again to reiterate the point, not much is known about Melbourne, so take this guide with a grain of salt.

THE LOCALS

NOTABLE TYPES

The Smashed Av

The Dinks

Lads and Lasses

The Post-War Wog

The Modern Wog

The Concrete Cowboy

THE
SMASHED AV

LIKES

Smashed av & coffee

Writing blogs

Recording podcasts

Everything about the 1970s, except the way women, gays and black people were treated

Gentrification

DISLIKES

The housing market

Working at the same place for more than 18 months

Coppers

ALSO KNOWN AS

Hipsters

Stone & Wood Socialists

Inner-city Elites

Millennials

OFTEN FOUND

West End (Brisbane)

Redfern (Sydney)

Fitzroy (Melbourne)

Smashed avocado on sourdough, or better yet, smashed av on highly processed gluten-free bread, has become a symbol for the inner-city bubble. So much so that it has become a demographic in itself.

The Smashed Av is a worldly, compassionate, open-minded student of contemporary urban Australia – be that a tertiary student or a YouTube surfer.

The Smashed Av is usually on the frontline of gentrification. Their desperation when it comes to navigating the \Australian rental market results in six-person share houses in the dodgier streets of this country's remaining inner-city ghettos.

The Smashed Av's migration to inner areas, such as Redfern and West End, is often followed by the yummy mummy, Greens-voting baby boomer and waves of coffee shops and bakeries.

Occupationally, Smashed Avs like to refer to themselves as 'Collarless', meaning they aren't working in either recognised trades or professional industries. 'Creative Freelancer' is another term used to describe the Hipster's occasional work in videography and content writing. A far more accurate word to describe their profession is 'Bartender'.

With a uniquely streamlined intake of news, from an array of city-centric online publications, the Hipster is seldom educated on the many issues faced by Australians who don't live within their 20-kilometre radius of pokie-free pubs, which serve American style hamburgers and other contrived foods that avoid looking anything like a chicken schnitzel.

So blinded are they by the issues of lock-out laws and marijuana legislation, the Smashed Av is nearly illiterate when it comes to the national debate about pressing socio-economic issues outside of their bubble – such as drought, traffic and the scourge of crystal meth.

While many argue that being offended is actually the Smashed Av's preferred co-curricular activity, they're also known for their love of non-mainstream sports such as bike polo and Frisbee. They also enjoy apologising to their friends for not being able to make their struggling band's latest gig.

Unlike most of the demographics outlined in this book, the Smashed Av is more a transient phase for the nation's youth, as opposed to a social class.

While many of them feel they'll live this free-spirited life of MDMA and Tame Impala forever, it's a lifestyle that's not sustainable. The cost of inner-city living eventually results in the trendy Millennial being forced by their parents to take a job in a secure industry that can be vaguely associated with creativity, like marketing or event planning.

THE
DINKS

OFTEN FOUND

New Farm (Qld)

Byron Bay (NSW)

Darlinghurst (NSW)

Erskineville (NSW)

St Kilda (Vic)

South Yarra (Vic)

Semaphore (SA)

LIKES

Mardi Gras

Renovating

Tank tops

Massive Sunday sessions

ALSO KNOWN AS

Queens

Gays

Hommusexuals

DISLIKES

Not being able to get married

Other gay people in their non-gay social circle

Tony Abbott

The Dink (Dual Income No Kids) represents some of Australia's wealthiest inner-city occupants. They are the white-collar elite, with two steady male-grade salaries.

Due to the almost impossible obstacles placed in front of same-sex couples who dream of raising children, the homosexual population of Australia is often seen to be building their wealth beyond the imagination of those who are weighed down by the costs of maternity leave, paternity leave and raising children.

While many have been successful in having kids, the inner-city gay populations, which most non-Dinks are exposed to, are the laughing tribes of men outside trendy cafes with well-sculpted calves and well-groomed pets.

Much like the Jet-Ski-Owner and the Modern Wog, the Dink is renowned for their impulse purchases and disposable income, although they're not exactly as big on jewellery or water sport.

The Australian arts, theatre, homeware, luxury motorcar and furniture industries are well aware of the cash cow that exists in this country's rainbow belts, and have been gay-friendly since the 80s.

In a world that so badly wants to group this community with other minorities – identified by alternative lifestyles, sexual orientations and gender politics – the Dinks have marched to their own drum and avoided all acronyms altogether.

While many do have blue-collar lesbian friends, somehow the Dink rejects the title of 'LGBTQI Community'. Many believe this is because their unrelenting male libido has forced this demographic into forging themselves a place in Australian society, with or without the others.

Another reason why the Dink may have split from the pack is the fact that, ultimately, most of them are pretty happy to make use of what remaining privileges they enjoy as white males.

Despite still carrying a list of reasonable demands when it comes to equal rights, Dinks have not been seen protesting the streets since the 70s.

Their seemingly detached attitude from politics leaves the rest of the population thinking that the money may have gone to their heads – with the majority of Dinks appearing to be more interested in buying a holiday home than standing on the picket line.

However, what many seem to underestimate is the work that goes into taking down Australian political and institutional homophobia from the inside. Even a quick glance at any meeting for the Young Liberal Party will confirm that the days are numbered for red-nosed straight white conservatives.

It appears that Australia's dark history of male stoicism, poofter-bashing and toxic masculinity has spawned an army of cold-hearted sleeper cells, who've risen to the top of Australian law firms, broker firms, political parties and media companies with the aim of doing two things: renovating terrace houses and smashing the straightriarchy.

And this country is all out of un-renovated terrace houses.

THE
LADS AND LASSES

OFTEN FOUND

Redlands Bay (Qld)

Caboolture (Qld)

Liverpool (NSW)

Coburg (Vic)

Other rough suburban areas of Australia

ALSO KNOWN AS

Eshays /Adlays /Asslays

DISLIKES

Mum dropping them off in front of everyone

Ticket inspectors / Coppers

LIKES

Nautica

Polo

Nike TNs

Knowing what you're looking at

Knowing if you've got a smoke

Lads and Lasses are a relatively new cultural phenomenon for Australian youth (and creepy middle-aged blokes with one-too-many tattoos on their faces).

The culture spawned from a wave of culturally frustrated and disenfranchised young white people, who don't like behaving in a way that authority figures would deem acceptable.

Initially starting as nothing more than a niche fashion style in Melbourne and Sydney's urban sprawl, the subculture eventually spread to other cities and towns around the country – anywhere that people enjoy dealing drugs and getting into violent confrontations at train stations.

Identifiable by their choice of pocketless football shorts and tracksuits, this community is well known for their love of collared shirts and sailing headwear brands supposedly representing wealth – similar to their Northern Hemisphere cousins, the Burberry-laden 'Chavs'.

Lads and Lasses are also inclined to use bumbags to carry their phones, wallets, saddie bags and cigarettes – making them the only other demographic outside paramedics and aged pensioners to utilise the 'fanny-pack'.

Since its inception, Lad culture has been underrepresented in mainstream media – who seem unable to see that Australian youth gang activity isn't limited to just South Sudanese and Middle-Eastern youths.

As for the non-mainstream media, Lads and Lasses are well documented on YouTube, Instagram and in *The Betoota Advocate*.

Like the Bodgies, Widgies, Skinheads and Bikies of decades gone, this community is made up of a small portion of criminally minded individuals – and a large community of people who enjoy being mistaken for criminally minded individuals.

Lads and Lasses are credited with the revival of pig Latin in the Australian vernacular. What was initially a way of talking about naughty things in front of teachers has eventually become a sort of pidgin dialect. Oday you antway any ingerspay, adlay?

Like most other demographics, females are their backbone. Their unrelenting use of swear words and heavy application of mascara makes for strong leaders, who are never shy of 'geeing up' their nutcase male partners or friends onto some lippy c—t at a house party.

While Lad culture is gradually being more and more represented in professional sport, through the likes of David Klemmer and Dustin Martin, their idols are mostly 'lad rap' musicians. Such as the iconic South-West Sydney YouTube sensation MC Ker$er, who mainstream radio simply refuse to play, but still manages to top the ARIA charts each year in album sales. Australian rock group DMA's are also closely associated with the Lad community.

THE POST-WAR WOG

OFTEN FOUND

Earlwood (Sydney)

South Brisbane

All of Melbourne

Ingham (Qld)

Townsville (Qld)

Stanthorpe (Qld)

Wollongong (NSW)

Broken Hill (NSW)

Griffith (NSW)

ALSO KNOWN AS

New Australians

Wops

Eyeties

LIKES

Any well-known person who shares their ethnic background

Massive weddings

Concrete

DISLIKES

Modern migrants

The state of their home country

Coppers

The origins of the word 'Wog' are fiercely debated. Some say it's an acronym for 'Workers of Government', which came about when early Greek and Italian migrants were working on government migration schemes such as the Snowy Mountains Scheme. Others believe it stands for 'Western Oriental Gentleman' – a much nicer way of justifying a racial slur.

However, the actual Australian Wog community believes it means: 'Wonder of God'.

Once upon a time, this word was used by Australians to provoke the Southern European migrant. It was a word that could make the passionate Mediterranean blood boil, especially if it came from some 'Skippy Poof'.

However, as is often the story with multiculturalism, their ability to build a fortune far bigger than that of most of their white neighbours in a single generation means it's now a term linked with success and tax avoidance.

Like all waves of migrants, the Post-war Wogs had to spend a good couple of decades assuring the rest of Australia that the blokes shooting each other and stealing cars weren't representative of their whole community. Eventually, after delivering some talented footballers across all codes, they were accepted as real Aussies. The fact that the food they brought with them was fucking delicious also helped.

Architecturally, this community has contributed greatly to urban Australia. With a love of heavily concreted backyards, the Post-war Wog is easily identified by their heavy water usage.

Often referred to as 'the Greek broom', the Southern European practice of hosing down driveways has been a hot topic for local politicians for many years now, with a large contingent of non-Greek Australians complaining that the decadent practice is a blatant and unnecessary waste of resources. But, as most wogs will tell you, they're just jealous because their own backyard is covered in all that tacky grass.

While initially staunch Labor voters, most Post-war Wogs started to steer towards the Liberal Party after starting their own businesses and making some money. Conservative Australian politics also resonated with their new-found hatred of lazy younger people, and other migrants.

The Post-war Wog is well known for the merciless indifference they show towards the waves of migrants who came after them. A true sign of cultural assimilation is their 'pull the ladder up' attitude – and their inability to see themselves in the Vietnamese and Arabs who've arrived in the decades after them (see: The Modern Wog).

THE MODERN WOG

OFTEN FOUND

Logan (Qld)

Sunshine (Vic)

Punchbowl (NSW)

Point Piper (NSW)

ALSO KNOWN AS

Persons of Middle Eastern Appearance

Mussies

DISLIKES

Coppers / Cronulla

LIKES

Hip-hop clubs

Illegally modified street-racing vehicles

Gym supplements

Muzzing / Music festivals

The Modern Wog is one of this country's most unrecognised economic contributors. Much like their post-war predecessors, an instinct for entrepreneurship, paired with an undying love of glamour and glitz, has provided a stimulatory cash injection into the contemporary Australian economy.

After the success of Post-war Wogs, as well as Malcolm Fraser's wave of Vietnamese refugees (who introduced the pork roll banh mi to our industrial estate bakeries), our nation's immigration policies began expanding to include nations in Northern Africa, Eastern Mediterranean and the Middle East. These people came to be known as the Modern Wog.

This community's fine taste in brand-new tracksuits, muscle shirts, jewellery, sports cars, cocktail dresses, haircuts, nightclubs and gym supplements is making millionaires out of the sort of people 'old money' families never would have dreamed about associating with 20 years ago – let alone be forced to live next to.

With burning ambition, they've managed to carve out lives for themselves on both sides of our cities. From hanging out at train stations in Sydney's Wild West to proudly parking their Range Rovers outside their palatial Eastern Suburbs mansions – next to old white neighbours who'd tried to stop the boats they came here on.

Unfortunately for the Modern Wog, their assimilation into Australian society was somewhat hindered by an incident in New York City sixteen or so years ago. Their lives and successes in this country have been a topic for political populism ever since.

Until the Smashed-Av community's lumberjack renaissance – which saw an increase in facial hair for young inner-city men – a bearded adult male was perceived to be as political as a woman wearing a scarf, unless that woman was a Christian nun.

While contemporary Australian Muslims have received praise for managing to not conduct themselves in a way that would see them

investigated by a Royal Commission, they've also received a lot of flak for a very small number of troubled youths who've chosen violent religious extremism over listening to rap music.

Another tag often given to the Modern Wog is the crime tag. As our cities' organised crime outfits evolve from the Carl Williams and Roger Rogersons, media outlets have developed a taste for the bloodletting caused by reporting hyphenated Arabic names, especially when associated with motorcycles, drive-by shootings and religion.

Such is the hysteria surrounding the Muslim faith, regardless of how strictly it's followed, that many of Australia's xenophobes simply refuse to acknowledge this community's achievements and loyalty to Australia.

The facts still remain, kebabs and baklava are fucking delicious, and the highest-scoring footballer to ever play rugby league – Hazem 'El Magic' El Masri – has never had a beer and spends a lot of time in mosques.

THE CONCRETE COWBOY

OFTEN FOUND

Ryan's Bar (Sydney)

The Oaks Hotel (Sydney)

Friday's Riverside (Brisbane)

The Surf Club, Mooloolaba (Qld)

The Surf Club, Noosa (Qld)

Pacific Hotel, Yamba (NSW)

ALSO KNOWN AS

Pitt Street Farmers

Queen Street Cowboys

DISLIKES

Working in different industries
to their dads

The Labor Party

Coppers

LIKES

Getting out bush

Talking about getting out bush

Unnecessarily heavy duty utes
in the city

Rugby union

Failed business ventures in their
twenties

Country music

Despite the fact that he's able to incorporate a Toyota LandCruiser, moleskin trousers, R.M. Williams boots and Champion Ruby tobacco into his daily routine – the Concrete Cowboy is seldom seen further west than his city's car-dealership mile.

But he's more than willing to tell you about the time he bit the bullet and drove out to the Roma Races, and another time he went roo-shooting out near Moree.

The 'Queen Street Cowboys', or 'Pitt Street Farmers', are a community of professional men who emulate the culture and attire of regional Australians, in an attempt to look more worldly, capable and masculine.

Usually spotted working in mid- to high-level corporate finance and legal positions in the CBDs across the east coast of Australia, the Concrete Cowboy spends his free time drinking cans of mass-produced beer on timber-deck stilt houses, while listening to Powderfinger, Silverchair, Jimmy Barnes and, eventually, Slim Dusty at the back end of the night.

While the Concrete Cowboy is also found in Melbourne, Adelaide and Perth, the population is more present in rugby union heartlands.

Reds, Waratahs and Brumbies scarves are often seen wrapped around their M.J. Bale tailored collared shirts on weekends – a colourful inclusion to the earthy tones of their moleskin trousers and dark leather dress boots.

The Concrete Cowboy's half-hearted claims to love rugby league are usually only brought to light during the annual State of Origin series, or when in actual conversation with real people from the bush.

The female version of the Concrete Cowboy – much less vocal about their bush fetishism – are much more likely to end up starting a life on the land.

The commonly accepted title for the female equivalent is 'Acre Chaser' – due to their blinding ambition to land themselves a grazier with a lot of wide-open space.

While not nearly as insecure as the Concrete Cowboy, the Acre Chaser is just as well known for their commitment to regional outfitters – their most notable accessory being the bright pink agribus-branded caps they wear to club football matches.

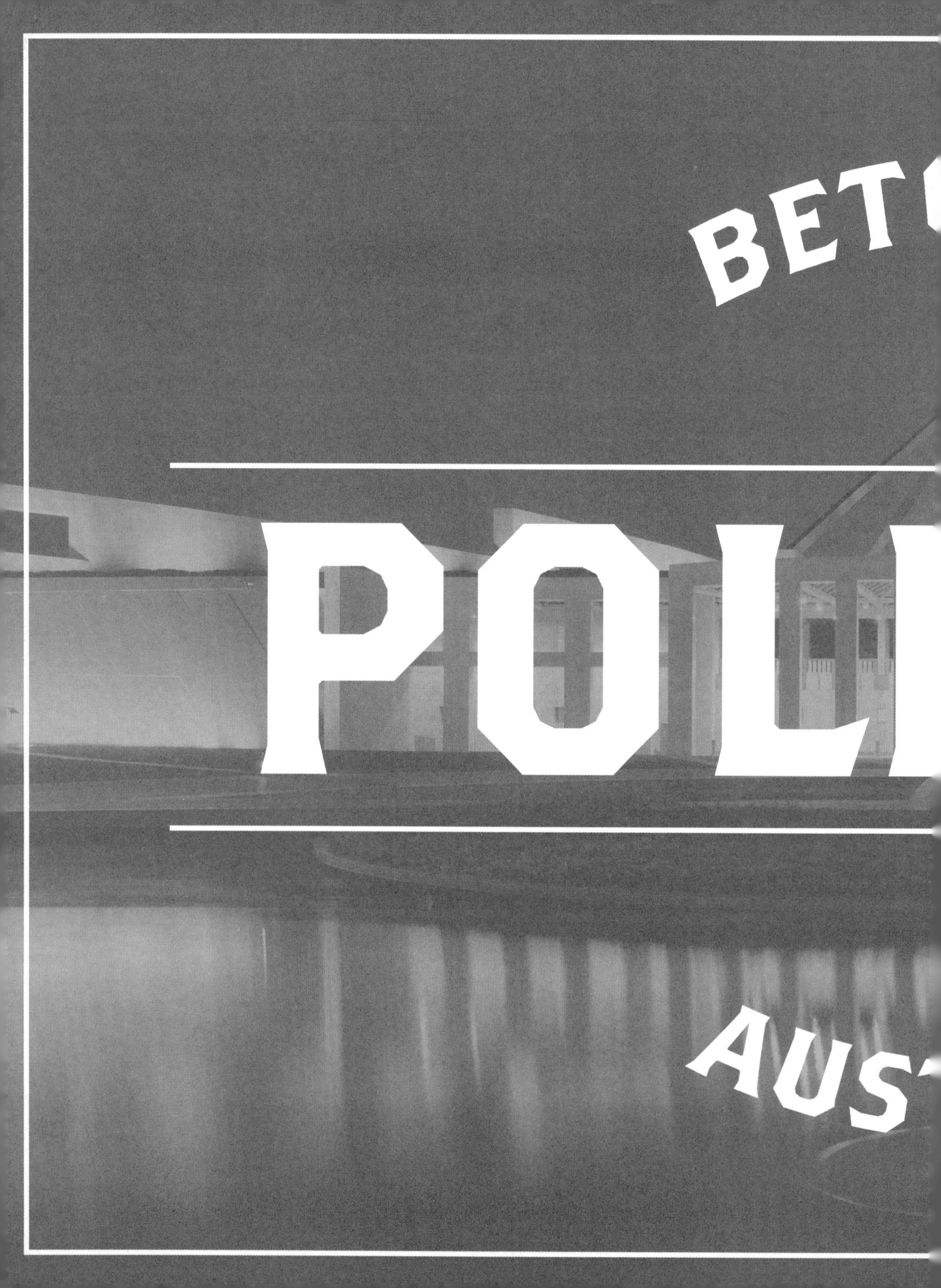
BET
POL
AUS

TA'S

TICS

ALIA

THE PARTIES

'The most intense hatreds are not between political parties but within them.'
– Phillip Adams

MAJORS

One Nation

Katter's Australia Party

The Greens

The ALP

The National Party

The Liberal Party

The Australian Democrats

MINORS

Xenophon / Derryn Hinch / Lambie / Australian Conservatives / Liberal Democrats

While politics is not something that dominates kitchen table talk across the Diamantina Shire, it's worth getting your head around the different tribes you can expect to find across the country.

It's no lie that Betoota's residents treat politics the same way that we treat religion – it's something you only have to pay attention to once every three or so years, when someone dies, gets married or an election is called.

It is important to know that – in some of the more underprivileged, or just plain boring, regions around Australia – politics is something that people cling to. Either as a pivotal force in their day-to-day struggles, or as something that makes them feel intelligent and important.

While Betoota, historically, has been a safe seat for the National Party of Australia for decades, it's mainly because our town is so self-sufficient that the only thing these political blokes need to do is show up to the races once a term and get pissed.

As boring as Q&A is, when attempting to live in the inner-city areas of Australia, it is very important to know which incredibly intelligent lefty said what. And if, for some reason, you find yourself living in the godforsaken Northern suburbs of Melbourne, Brisbane or Sydney, it's also handy to know which racial minority 2GB has been sticking the boot into recently.

Parliament House, atop Capital Hill, has one of the highest instances of robust irreverence anywhere in the country. The old one was much nicer.

IF, FOR SOME REASON, YOU FIND YOURSELF LIVING IN THE GODFORSAKEN NORTHERN SUBURBS OF MELBOURNE, BRISBANE OR SYDNEY, IT'S HANDY TO KNOW WHICH RACIAL MINORITY 2GB HAS BEEN STICKING THE BOOT INTO RECENTLY.

ONE NATION

ALSO KNOWN AS

Sunrise Live-Cross Talent

Nationalsozialistische Deutsche Arbeiterpartei

PROMINENT FIGURES

Pauline Hanson, Federal Senator, Queensland

Malcolm Roberts, Federal Senator, Queensland

Brian Whatshisface, Federal Senator, NSW

Peter Somethingorother, Federal Senator, Western Australia

David Koch, Pauline Hanson's Publicist, Channel 7 Sunrise

One Nation is a far-right-wing political party, which was formed in Ipswich, Queensland in 1997, by a fish-and-chip shop owner, Pauline Hanson, and her advisor, David Oldfield, a wealthy North Shore Baby Boomer. The party began after Pauline Hanson was brushed from the Liberal Party of Australia just before the 1996 federal election because of comments she'd made about blackfellas.

Pauline Hanson limped through her first term in the lower house and saw a brief flutter of success after getting the nation's Jet-Ski Owners excited by her fear-inciting speeches about Asians taking their jobs and First Australians getting an extra helping hand in life that they don't deserve.

Her populist brand of politics saw her win more than 11 seats in the 1998 Queensland state election. However, most of the candidates were inexperienced and had put about as much thought into the job as the people who voted for them did.

They eventually disbanded and Pauline Hanson went to jail for registering the party fraudulently and for inappropriate fund raising.

From here, the party chugged along with just the one consistent state seat in Queensland, held by Rosa Lee Long, whose husband was of Chinese descent until she was voted out in 2009.

ONE NATION STRONGHOLDS

Regional coastal Qld
City-outskirts Qld
Regional coastal NSW
City-outskirts NSW
Regional coastal WA
City-outskirts WA

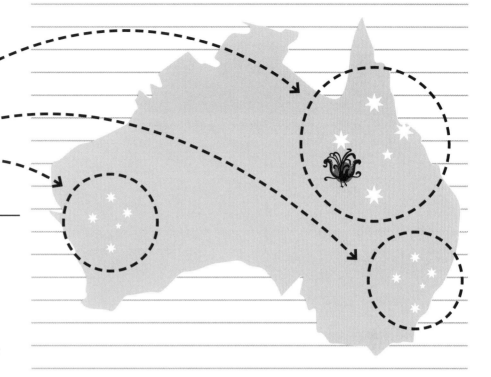

elow: Party figurehead Pauline
anson wishes Australians would
nderstand what she is trying to do for
. She is trying to protect us.

But that wasn't the end of the xenophobic xenophone. After her release from jail and a dabble in the reality TV limelight, Pauline Hanson went down the same path as Donald J. Trump.

She started with *Dancing with the Stars*, and then made her way to *The Celebrity Apprentice Australia*, before she secured a recurring role as a paid 'terror expert' on Channel 7's 'Sunrise'.

But in 2016, after a spate of terrorist attacks across Europe and a wave of human dispossession in Syria, the iron was hot.

Like a phoenix, Pauline Hanson's One Nation Party rose from the ashes of Asian migration and Aboriginal race baiting, only to find new, more terrifying targets: Muslims, African teenagers, single mums experiencing domestic violence and vaccinations.

Let's do it all again!

KATTER'S AUSTRALIAN PARTY

ALSO KNOWN AS

The Good Old Party

KAP

Old Labor

PROMINENT FIGURES

Bob Katter (Federal MP for Kennedy, Party Leader)

Robbie Katter (State MP for Mount Isa, State Leader, Son of Bob)

Shane Knuth (State MP for Charters Towers)

James Blundell (Country music singer, former Senate candidate)

Katter's Australian Party (KAP) is a nationalistic agrarian-socialist and protectionist political party, founded on the key personality traits of their leader, maverick bush politician Bob Katter II.

Like the Katter family, the Katter Party has a tight grip above the Queensland line of Capricornia and further west to the Gulf Country. The party itself can be best described by understanding its founder.

Bob Katter was born in the Outback Queensland town of Cloncurry, to a pioneering family of Murri, Arabic, Jewish and Irish Convict background.

His father, Robert Carl Katter, was from a family of Lebanese migrants who anglicised their family name from 'Khattar'. Bob senior is remembered as one of the founding investors in QANTAS and served as a Labor politician both for

Cloncurry Council and as a Federal MP for the Kennedy Electorate, like his son.

The current 'Honest Bob' Katter has stated that his tertiary education in Brisbane and subsequent political career only came after he was forced to admit that he would never play professional rugby league. It was also during his time at University of Queensland that he was arrested for throwing eggs at the Beatles during their first few minutes on Australian soil.

He started public life as the State Member for Mount Isa, a seat his son Robbie now holds. His staunch anti-Southern sentiment can be traced back to his tutelage under the iconic Sir Joh Bjelke-Petersen – a man capable of spinning far-taller yarns than Bob himself … even when in front of a judge.

His Federal career began with the National Party, before they got too soft and forced him to serve in the same seat as an Independent. In 2011, he rallied all his best bull-shitters from the bush and formed what is now known as KAP.

Similarly to the iconic big-hatted country music singer Slim Dusty, Katter's larger-than-life personality is one that ironically appeals to both blackfellas and white supremacists.

Bob Katter has for many years been a vocal supporter of black Australia – often identifying as a 'Murri' himself – and encourages people of all backgrounds to try their luck in the Gulf, except for the terrorists.

However, for the Southerner, Katter's entire political career is essentially defined by one comment: 'I'll walk backwards from Bourke if there are any gays in North Queensland.' – Bob Katter MP, 1989

The Hon Bob Katter is the president of the Backward Walking Association of Mount Isa and frequently challenges people to backward walking competitions.

KATTER'S
STRONGHOLDS

West Qld
Far-West Qld
North Qld
Far-North Qld
Far North-West Qld

THE GREENS

ALSO KNOWN AS

The Australian Greens

Rich Man's Labor

Your Daughter's Hippy Phase

PROMINENT FIGURES

Bob Brown (former Party Leader)

Richard Di Natale (current Party Leader, Federal Senator)

The Australian Greens is a left-wing political party which was founded as an alternative choice for people who care about the planet, cherish human rights and enjoy talking over other people at dinner parties.

With roots that can be traced back to the original tree-huggers in the Tasmania timber towns, the Greens were formed as a coalition of different chapters from the industrial left and nuclear disarmament groups from across the country.

Their stances on decriminalising drugs, ecological sustainability, not going to war and not imprisoning people unnecessarily have made them the target for conservative commentators. This has resulted in the rise of pit-bull progressive politicians within the party, who play on the front foot against rivals, shock jocks and corporations.

Unfortunately, this also has affected their internal party politics. With a political movement based around such a broad list of aims, the infighting between aggressively confident party members is prolific.

The warring factions essentially boil down to Baby Boomer communists versus university graduates who hate football.

Despite having core 'hinterland' supporters, who are as reliable as

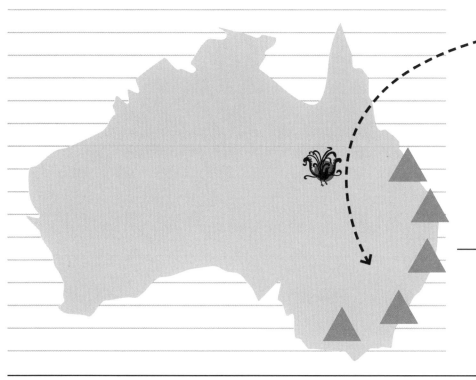

GREENS STRONGHOLDS

Tasmania
Inner-city Sydney
Inner-city Melbourne
Inner-city Brisbane
Byron Bay (NSW)
Eumundi (Qld)

Below: Senator Richard Di Natale [left] and Bob Brown [right] are two political heavyweights that together equal the wealth and influence of a Nationals backbencher.

their dreadlocks and torn up Tally-Hos, the party entered the 21st century with a growing inner-city support base, which they had not accounted for.

Following the late 90s trend, which saw rich people deciding to move out of the suburbs and back into once working-class urban areas, the Greens had at their disposal a powerful faction of people wealthy and isolated enough to care about their policies.

However, as we learned from the US Trump election, this 'Inner-city Leftie' tag has come to hurt the progressives, as their core 'hinterland' supporters can often feel detached from the lawyer haircuts and big words of Chardonnay Socialists.

Since the 2016 Australian Federal Election, the Greens have 9 senators and 1 MP, 23 elected representatives across State and Territory parliaments, and more than 100 local councillors – as well as hundreds of sympathising independents who were too scared to wear the armband.

AUSTRALIAN LABOR PARTY

ALSO KNOWN AS

ALP

The Labs

PROMINENT FIGURES

Bill Shorten (Leader, MP)

Anthony Albanese (former Deputy Leader, enemy of Bill Shorten)

Tanya Plibersek (Deputy Leader, bad girl of Australian politics)

Sam Dastyari (Federal Senator, party jester)

Kevin Rudd (former Prime Minister, enemy of Bill Shorten)

Julia Gillard (former Prime Minister, enemy of Rudd and Shorten)

The Australian Labor Party is one of Australia's two major political parties. It formed as a conglomerate of several industrial-left movements that were operating across the country in the late 1800s.

While many inner-city communist factions lay claim to founding the party, it is commonly acknowledged among historians that the ALP was first established by Outback Queensland shearers, who were refusing to go to work one day in 1891.

From day one, the party has been a politically fluid organisation made up of barely functional rivalries. One reason for this is the diverse issues that the party faces as a whole, across a range of geographical electorates and economic classes. Another reason is that there is not one member – at local, state or federal level – who does not secretly dream of being Prime Minister.

However, despite a long history of backstabbing and ideological hijacking, the Labor Party is best remembered for leading Australia into a modern global economy – with two solid prime ministerships under Bob Hawke (1983–91) and eventually the former's deputy, the unashamed Francophile Paul Keating (1991–96).

Between the two, the country was run by the same political party for

Bill Shorten is a person who is the Leader of the Opposition. Not much else is known about this man.

more than 13 years, one of the longest stints in recent memory. Hawke's beer-swilling masculinity and ability to name the entire Australian cricket side was perfectly complemented by Keating's love of French Empire mantel clocks and big words.

Both contributed to the development of Medicare, land rights and the infantile stages of the worldwide web.

Even though, like most high-ranking Labor contemporaries the two actually hated each other, they were able to put progress and longevity ahead of their burning ambitions – a political trait that hasn't been seen since, in any of the major parties.

After entering the 21st century with three rapid-fire Labor Governments in under five years – simply known as the 'Rudd, Gillard, Rudd' years – the Labor Party has succumbed to the instant gratification of social media and polling software. It's a political strategy not yet proven to result in longevity.

Like a teenage girl changing her display picture on Facebook, the party is constantly convincing itself that it could do with a better leader, or reminiscing about recently backstabbed leaders, or going to the media behind their current leader's back.

The ALP's main opposition isn't much better when it comes to continuity or change, but the Liberal Party hasn't yet stooped as low as reinstating a previously ousted Prime Minister.

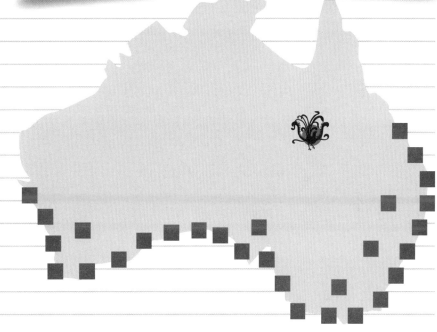

ALP STRONGHOLDS

Industrial waterfront suburbs
Industrial outskirt suburbs
Generational working-class suburbs
Yuppie areas that are too proud to go full Green

THE NATIONAL PARTY

ALSO KNOWN AS

The National Party of Australia / The National Party /The Nationals / The Nats / Nats / Nat

PROMINENT FIGURES

Barnaby Joyce (Deputy Prime Minister of Australia, Leader of the Nationals)

Fiona Nash (Deputy Leader of the Nationals)

John Anderson (former Deputy PM, former Leader of the Nationals)

Mark Vaile (former Deputy PM, former Leader of the Nationals)

Mark Coulton (Federal MP for Parkes)

Ralph Hunt (former Deputy Leader of the Nationals)

Sir Joh Bjelke-Petersen (former Premier of Queensland)

Traditionally representing farmers, graziers and rural voters, the National Party has its federal roots in the former Australian Country Party, founded in 1920. They were briefly National Country Party from 1975, before taking its current name in the months after the 1982 Falklands War.

And since then, their city cousins have paraded them around the country in an attempt to appear in touch with the working man. Often heard before they're seen, the clip-clopping of Baxter boots comes hand in hand with visiting the Nationals wing of Parliament House. Their Liberal coalition counterparts have all been issued with a pair of R.M. Williams boots for when they have to go and see a National Party member in his office.

Unlike other members in the House of Representatives, the Nationals are expected to walk in both worlds. They should feel as at home shaking the hands of world leaders and high-powered businessmen as they do in the bush.

However, while it's the Nationals who sleep on the Liberal couch when they come down for the cricket, it's the Liberals who sleep in the National

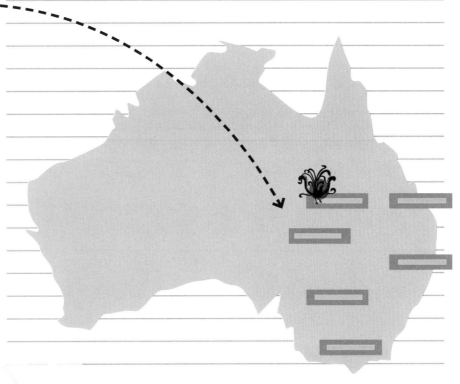

NATIONALS STRONGHOLDS

**Western NSW
South-West Qld
New England
NSW North Coast
Far-Western Victoria
Far-Eastern Victoria
Northern Victoria**

Below: The Deputy Prime Minister and Nationals leader Barnaby Joyce [below] was once laughed out of a Sydney General Pants store for asking if they had any Cowboy Cut Wranglers.

guestroom when they want to come up for the long weekend and shoot some animals to death for sport.

But putting Christopher Pyne on the headbail would simply be asking too much.

One unique aspect of the party, which even the most tie-dyed, septum-pierced, Green-voting lunatic can agree on, is that they don't backflip on much – even if it means using foreign investment to create jobs and growth in regional areas, whether it's in mining, coal-seam gas, agriculture or anything else.

It's a fairly transparent party, which operates on the old-country notion that you're only worth as much as your word.

Our local representative in Canberra, at the time of print, is Liberal–National the Hon. David Littleproud. Though he's bound by name to the Liberals, Littleproud identifies more with the National side of the coalition.

The man embodies what it means to vote National, as does the Leader, Barnaby Joyce. It means a quiet determination to shake a hand properly, look a person in the eye and tell them how it's going to be.

But despite all those the National Party represents – the graziers, farmers and rural voters – the Prime Minister owns more cattle than the whole party put together.

Food for thought.

THE LIBERAL PARTY OF AUSTRALIA

ALSO KNOWN AS

The Fiberals

The Right Party

Menzies' Revenge

PROMINENT FIGURES

Malcolm Turnbull (Prime Minister of Australia)

Tony Abbott (former Prime Minister of Australia)

Julie Bishop (Deputy Leader of the Liberal Party)

Christopher Pyne (Federal Member for Sturt)

The Liberal Party is the largest and most dominant party in the Coalition with the National Party of Australia, the Country Liberal Party of the Northern Territory and the Liberal National Party (LNP) of Queensland.

For all intents and purposes, the LNP of Queensland will be part of the Liberal Party of Australia in this brief description.

The modern-day Liberal Party was founded on Van Morrison's birthday, 31 August 1945 – a mere three weeks after the atomic bomb was dropped on Hiroshima, Japan.

To this day, it still spruiks the economic liberalism that was born in the years after World War II. It's often seen as the sensible, stable vote. A vote that your parents and local business owners would do. A vote for stability and the status quo.

As the old adage goes: if you vote Liberal under the age of 30, you have no heart. If you vote Liberal over the age of 30, you have no brains.

In recent years, stability has been the major drawcard for the party, even though they've only changed their leader once – which is to be expected in a modern Australian democracy.

However, with stability comes the Jesus. Christianity has soaked through the party like beer soaks through the

Below: The Prime Minister, Malcolm Turnbull, is the leader of the Liberal Party. He once did a SWOT analysis on the economic benefits one might receive from drinking yard glasses over pints.

carpet of your favourite sports bar. A vote for the Liberal Party is a vote for the Jesus and everything that He and His Dad stand for, which typically doesn't align with modern values.

Although the Bible states that any man wearing a garment of mixed fibres ought to be stoned to death, Liberal staffers have seemingly ignored that aspect of their holy text. Nearly all wear suits made with at least 15 per cent polyester, as stipulated by party bylaws.

However, for all the faults and mishaps endured and suffered by the Liberal Party and, in turn, the Australian people, they've proven themselves to be economic realists. The party rewards financial bravery; they encourage people to get out and have a go in the modern marvel that is capitalism. They only want the best for you.

It's easy to spend your life sailing around the safe harbour, working for a boss, who also has a boss, who also has a boss. The tastiest fruit in life is at the top of the tree and if you don't want to climb, work and battle, then learn to be content with the over-ripe slop that falls to the ground on the first day of summer.

To live the way the Liberal Party wants you to live, untie yourself from the rocks of economic stability. Start your business and enjoy the tax breaks. Pull hard on the halyard of business and tack bravely out into the churning sea of the free-market economy.

Or you could just put your ugg boots on, curl up on the couch and laugh at the ignorant Liberal politicians showcased and lampooned every night on the ABC.

LIB STRONGHOLDS

Western, far-eastern, and north-eastern suburbs of Sydney
Western Australia
Eastern suburbs of Melbourne
North Queensland
Pyne's South Australia
Parts of New South Wales Coast and Hume Corridor
Capricornia

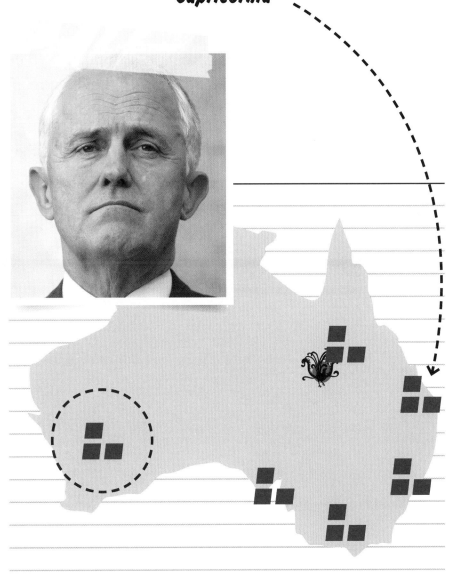

JACQUI LAMBIE NETWORK

ALSO KNOWN AS

Jacqui Lambie

PROMINENT FIGURES

Jacqui Lambie

The 2016 US Presidential Election will forever marvel and confuse analysts, commentators and voters – but Australians, of all people, should have seen it coming.

Three years earlier, a man with a big plane, a big suit and a big string of hotels did the same thing to our political system. His name was Clive Palmer.

The only thing that Trump did differently was to bring his own friends with him, unlike Palmer, who went scouring the suburbs and small towns for candidates and staffers to join

him in draining the political swamp. What he ended up with was the most obscure army of community members yet seen in the Australian political arena: the Palmer United Party.

While Palmer entered the lower house as MP for Fairfax on the Sunshine Coast, his biggest mark on the election was the three upper house senators gifted to Australia: former NRL star Glenn 'The Brick with Eyes' Lazarus, Chinese-Australian Perth businessman Dio Wang and Tasmanian ex-military super-mum Jacqui Lambie.

Along with his posse of political outsiders, Palmer was able to negotiate an alliance with the equally obscure Australian Motoring Enthusiast Party senator, Ricky Muir. Four senators and an MP meant Clive Palmer was now a very real player in Federal politics, for a few months anyway.

Then their deputy leader Lambie resigned from the party and went independent, shortly before Lazarus resigned from the party and went independent, leaving only Clive and Dio Wang to hold the fort. After a

JACQUI'S
STRONGHOLDS

Burnie, Tasmania

turbulent three years for Clive, in the party room and in the courtroom, the party failed to win a seat in the 2016 election.

Four years on, and Clive Palmer's habit of posting obscure memes to Facebook is the only remnant of the once-powerful PUP.

That, and Jacqui Lambie.

The underdog, who many thought was only elected off the back of Clive's media machine and his chequebook. The veteran-loving, politician-hating, unrefined lino-floor feminist retained her seat as a Federal senator with her new Jacqui Lambie Network party.

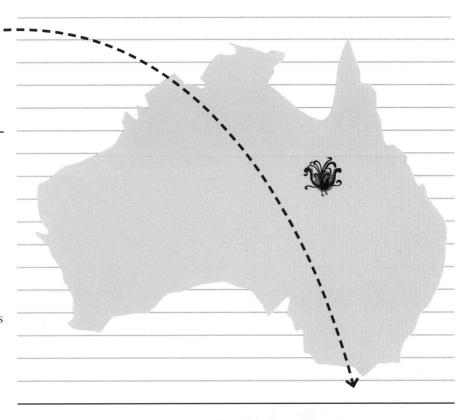

SHE HATES TERRORISTS, SHE HATES PEOPLE FUNDING TERRORISTS, SHE HATES SILVER-SPOON POLITICIANS AND SHE HATES WHINGERS.

The only Tasmanian willing to make sure that the entire political system puts her fellow 500,000 Tasmanians first in every political decision they make.

She hates terrorists, she hates people funding terrorists, she hates silver-spoon politicians and she hates whingers. She's lived the army life, she's lived the welfare life and she's raised a family in the backblocks. She knows more about Australia than any Sydney Uni graduate and she's not going anywhere.

Give it to 'em, Jacqui!

Deputy Prime Minister Barnaby Joyce, the bad boy of Australian agriculture.

Jacqui Lambie MP, the Queen of the Apple Isle.

Former Federal MP Clive Palmer, 100 kilos ago.

Senator Nick Xenophon talks with Errol and Clancy about pokie machines and Scientology, and why he fucking hates both of them.

Leader Of The New ALP, Anthony Alabanese MP. Just another degenerate South Sydney supporter.

Prime Minister Malcolm Turnbull having a little rest after a few jars of Betoota Bitter.

The Diamantina's Greatest Export

WESTERN QUEENSLAND'S FAVOURITE BEER

BETOOTA BITTER

USUALLY SERVED COLD

GET YOUR END IN

BBC

BETOOTA BOWLING CLUB

THE AUSTRALIAN DEMOCRATS

ALSO KNOWN AS

Dems

The New Libs

Don Chipp's Shipp

PROMINENT FIGURES

Don Chipp

Natasha Stott Despoja

Cheryl Kernot

Michael Macklin

Andrew Bartlett

The Australian Democrats, or the Democrats as they're known in political circles, is one of the most popular and influential medium-sized parties in the country – according to *The Betoota Advocate*.

Though they're not particularly popular in more regional areas such as our far-south-west and lesser parts of the interior, the Democrats have a long history of fence-sitting and trouble-making.

Founded in the 70s by maverick Liberal MP Don Chipp, the party prides itself on its centrist policies. What they are, nobody can really tell. While some agree that they now play second-fiddle to more populist environmental movements, the incorruptible core ethos of the Dems has allowed it to prosper and grow while others crash and burn by the wayside.

Until Greens senator Sarah Hanson-Young was elected to parliament at the 2007 general election, trailblazing Democrats senator Natasha Stott Despoja was the youngest person to be appointed to the federal senate. This didn't sit well with Despoja, who later went on to become leader of the party. Despite many calls for

Democrat heavyweights Michael Macklin [left] and John Cherry attending Wyatt Roy's 21st Birthday Party at AMF Bowling Belconnen.

Hanson-Young to produce her birth certificate, Stott Despoja ultimately retired from politics a year later.

However, the party didn't let that setback stop it from growing and gaining popularity.

Since 2008, the Australian Democrats have worked tirelessly to maintain their presence as the only snack-sized Australian political party dedicated to offering a centrist option for voters.

An interesting fact regarding the Democrats is that many political commentators, who have now chosen to remain anonymous, suggest that Malcolm Turnbull's brand of Liberal politics is almost the same as what the Democrats have offered for years. Although the Prime Minister has since found his feet politically, the many years he spent trying to make a purposeful and concrete decision within his own party and coming up with nothing displayed all the hallmarks of a true Australian Democrat. Those same commentators and analysts agree that Turnbull's latest budget is proof that at least one firm decision has been made, which flies in the face of the core Democrat belief that one can make political change by simply existing in the system.

DEMS
STRONGHOLDS

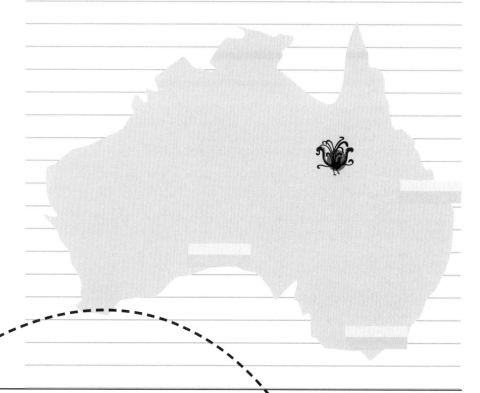

Brisbane
Melbourne
South Australia
Tasmania

THE MINOR
PARTIES

Cory Bernardi

Nick Xenophon

NICK XENOPHON TEAM

Similar to Katter's Australian Party, the Jacqui Lambie Network and the Palmer United Party, the Nick Xenophon Team is yet another Australian political party named after their leader, with policies based off the personal feelings of their leader.

While the party lists itself as completely 'centrist' – Nick Xenophon is no different to every other Australian man approaching his sixties. This means his political theology can change by the day, depending on his mood or what radio interview he last listened to.

That is, except when it comes to poker machines. Since day one, he has hated the fucking things and would gladly retire if it meant they were banned from our pubs and clubs forever.

Xenophon is a well-known political animal and is often viewed as a 'preference whisperer' in Federal politics. This means his constituents' issues are always paid full attention, and no one has ever publicly said that they dislike him.

THE AUSTRALIAN CONSERVATIVES

The Australian Conservatives is a far-right-wing religious political movement started by former Liberal senator Cory Bernardi – who defected from the governing party because he felt that the issues faced by privileged straight white men in the suburbs were not being prioritised by Malcolm Turnbull.

Bernardi was under the impression that his new party would become a major player in the Federal arena; that was, until his phone stopped ringing just weeks after his defection.

Their lack of headlines is something that Bernardi blames on a leftist media blacklist – but is more likely a result of his made-up issues. Like the banning of Easter? Or Christmas? Or that the Safe Schools programs encourage kids to become transgender against their will?

The party is similar to the ALP and One Nation, in that their sole reason for being is to criticise the decisions made by the Coalition – and the fact they might not exist come next election.

Derryn Hinch

DERRYN HINCH JUSTICE PARTY

As well as Xenophon, Lambie, Katter and Clive – the fifth and most recent 'personality party' to enter Parliament House is Derryn Hinch's Justice Party.

The party is based on the well-established opinions and sentiments held by former radio personality and reformed grogmonster, Derryn Hinch.

As far as anyone can tell, he exists purely to make life hard for sexual offenders, a well-documented pastime of Hinch since even before he entered politics. One that saw him sent to prison several times for naming child molesters and rapists on air, in contempt of court.

His dedication to Justice Reform and his pre-existing public profile helped him become elected into the senate in the 2016 election, making him the oldest Federal politician in Australia at 72. Apart from Pauline Hanson, Hinch is also the only other senator to have spent time in both prison and on *Dancing With the Stars*.

Left: Radio-shock-jock-turned-federal-senator Derryn Hinch led his Batman Justice Party to a shock victory last election under the pretence that he'd out sex offenders under parliamentary privilege.

LIBERAL DEMOCRATS

While Australia's middle-class female population are well known for their love of gossip magazines and astrology, the male equivalent is not as often discussed.

Similarly to *Woman's Day* and *New Idea*, it's born from a pointless obsession with the lives of the rich and powerful, as well as the staunch belief that fabricated theories created by overweight men on laptops are a gospel for how life works.

It's called social libertarianism, and it's what happens when undervalued white men get left alone for too long. The Liberal Democratic Party is the vehicle for this movement, and their leaders are guns-rights activist David Leyonhjelm and former Labor Party leader, Mark Latham.

This political party stands to remove politics from Australian life. Despite the fact that their party leader (Leyonhjelm) was accidentally elected by people who thought he was a Liberal Party candidate, they are 100 per cent of the belief that Australians agree with their policies that aim to legalise everything and be as offensive as possible at all times.

Below: The minor parties are always a hot bed of debate, anger, and tears.

MODERN AUSTRALIAN GRUB

'You can live off it, but it tastes like shit.' – Neil Perry

ICONIC DISHES

Chozzie

Butter Chicken

Pad Thai

Beef Stroganoff

Seafood

Pavlova

Corned Beef

Works Burger

Spag Bol

ustralia's inner-city cultural cringers would probably turn their nose up at the term 'Australian Cuisine', but in reality, the food that oozes Ochre is made up of good, honest hard-working morsels and dishes. Noted, we may not have fancy meals with hard-to-pronounce names such as 'Duck Confit', 'Pappardelle' or 'Foie Gras', but hooley dooley those 'Chiko Rolls' go alright, don't they! We have dishes that are steeped in the history of this great southern land. Dishes like damper, corned beef and meat pies. Dishes that should never be forgotten in this evolving new age of wilted and pickled modern dining.

Is there anything more Australiana than a big meat pie lathered in tomato sauce? It's funny to think about tradies on site in France, sitting down to a croissant with pâté and an espresso, isn't it? They have no idea what they're missing out on. Sitting on an empty upside-down bucket or white outdoor chair, the rustle of a white paper bag, the scalding heat of the first bite, and the wiping-away of sauce and meaty sludge from your face after you've polished that pie off. And, if you want to be technical, a meat pie isn't just a plain-old boring-old meat pie. You've got Steak and Pepper, Steak and Kidney, Steak and Cheese, and, let's not forget, the classic Chicken and Mornay.

In 2017 there are more places across Australia to feed your appetite than ever before. Walk down the happening streets in any of the major cities and towns, and you're guaranteed to find a fair variety of tucker originating from numerous places on this planet. From locally sourced bush tucker to Thai, Japanese, Italian, Korean, Chinese, Fusion and the canteens at local sporting games, just to name a few. The Melbournians can keep their

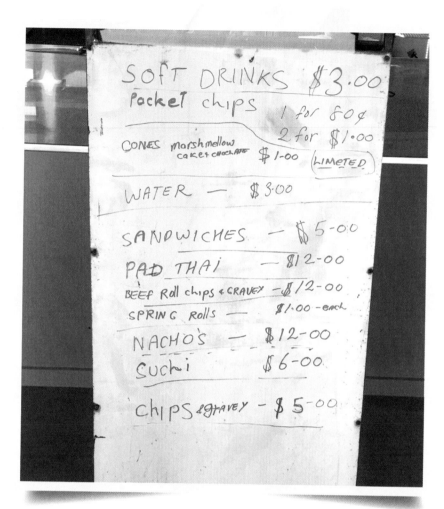

Above: The smorgasbord of local produce available at the Quilpie Diggers Race Club. Water was added this year as a gluten-free option.

deconstructed coffees and quinoa salads, because in a Betootan guide to good Aussie food, we simply aren't interested in it. However, it's extremely important to recognise the importance and value of cuisines that have been brought to Australia. Never has there been a better time to be alive. Yes, the whole foodie obsession has gone bloody mental – three different cooking shows on every single night and that social media thing is chockers with cooking videos – but holy Moses, stop and

think about how good it is that you can walk down the street at lunchtime and pick up a Pad Thai for under 10 clams. Yes, there will always be a place for meat pies, devon sandwiches and leftover corned beef. It's just that we now have the best of both worlds.

All in all, despite this country's newfound foodie obsession, there are a few quintessential dishes you just can't go past. We might be known for our lamingtons and Vegemite, but here is the list of absolute classic dishes. From Betoota to Brisbane, from Melbourne to Mackay and from Sydney to South Australia here is a guide to nine Aussie dishes/cuisines that get the seal of approval from Nan and Pop.

'CHOZZIE'

(CHINESE AUSSIE)

CULINARY INFLUENCES

China

RSL clubs

Other assorted cuisines from around the world

BEST SERVED WITH

Highbrow option:
Crown Lager

Working-class option:
Pure Blonde

BEST OCCASIONS

Night before a
family wedding

Family reunion

Birthday dinner

You'd be extremely hard-pressed to find a town or suburb in this country that doesn't have a good old-fashioned Chinese restaurant. Honestly, try and think about a place that doesn't have a 'Golden Sun', 'Mr Cho's' or 'Happy Restaurant'. Recognised by their bright red-and-gold awnings, set back against a usually white shopfront, these family-owned businesses have been feeding families, construction workers and

pensioners for as long as any of us can remember. It was the first time that Australians were encouraged to share their meals, although many didn't. Despite the fact that China is the most populous country in the world, and one of the largest by land area, their fantastic array of food has been narrowed down and perfected across this great southern land to a set menu. Chinese. Here in Betoota, one of the local jokes is: why isn't

the best Chinese dish going around technically Chinese, but Mongolian? Mongolian Lamb aside, a few other tasty dishes have become Chozzie institutions, such as Beef and Black Bean Sauce, Sweet and Sour Pork and, of course, Frieeeed Rice. From 14th birthday parties with your family to taking your grandparents out for dinner, there aren't many better ways of eating a copious amount of MSG than at your local Chozzie.

BEST SPOTS

August Moon Chinese Restaurant in Kyogle

2. Green Jade Asian Restaurant in Adelaide

3. Ying Chow Chinese Restaurant in Bunbury

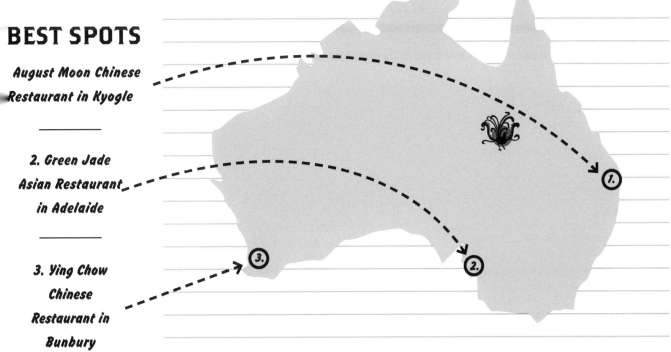

BUTTER CHICKEN

BEST SERVED WITH

Cheesy Naan

Victoria Bitter

KEY INGREDIENTS

Indian Spices

Butter

Chicken (or other bird)

Rice

BEST OCCASIONS

Hangovers

Watching movies or TV on the lounge

Looking at the menu in an Indian restaurant is one of the great pretences in Australian culture. It's when we study the four-page leaflet, pretending for a short period of time that we may order something other than Butter Chicken. Because there isn't a more unanimous fan favourite than this creamy treat. Put simply, everyone loves it. While the vast nation of China has been

IT'S WHEN WE STUDY THE FOUR-PAGE LEAFLET, PRETENDING FOR A SHORT PERIOD OF TIME THAT WE MAY ORDER SOMETHING OTHER THAN BUTTER CHICKEN.

narrowed down in Australia to a singular cuisine, the whole Indian subcontinent has been concentrated into a singular dish, Butter Chicken. The sweet buttery sauce complements a Cheesy Naan like nothing else. Many an Australian male will make Butter Chicken at home, but they'll all admit that they just can't do it anywhere near as well as our subcontinental Australian brothers.

Left: Butter Chicken has been a kitchen staple for generations. Its origins, however, are completely unknown.

BEST SPOTS

1. Masala Indian
Cuisine in Mackay

2. Flavours
of India
in Alice
Springs

3. Blue Lake
Tandoori Express
in Mt Gambier

PAD THAI

BEST PLACE TO FIND IT

Thai Me Up in Darlinghurst

Thai Tanic in Wolli Creek

N'Thai Sing in Terrigal

BEST SERVED WITH

Any beer or wine

Can of Coke

BEST OCCASIONS

Adult birthday parties
Short lunchbreaks

This tasty dish completes the Holy Trinity. Along with Butter Chicken and Mongolian Lamb, Pad Thai makes up the trio of ethnic dishes that Australians have had a long-running love affair with. Often served by a chirpy and giggling Thai lady, Pad Thai is the noodle-based stir-fry to order when you aren't sure what to order. While you'll have colleagues and friends aplenty who'll huff and say, 'Pad See Ew is wayyyyy

ALONG WITH BUTTER CHICKEN AND MONGOLIAN LAMB, PAD THAI MAKES UP THE TRIO OF ETHNIC DISHES THAT AUSTRALIANS HAVE HAD A LONG-RUNNING LOVE AFFAIR WITH.

better', we all know they're only trying to convince themselves. It's important to remember, if you feel under pressure to spice up your order, you don't need to stray from this staple, just mix it up and maybe order duck as your meat, or even seafood! This dish really is a universal one. For a quick-filling feed at 1 p.m. on a Wednesday or a BYO piss-up on a Saturday, Pad Thai has an incredible amount to offer.

BEEF STROGANOFF

A glass of water

The Footy Show

Any Anglo household

Tupperware containers

Thursdays
Fridays
When there isn't a whole lot else in the fridge

Beef Strog, as it's often known, is one of the most common Anglo household dishes round the country. And for good reason really. Who doesn't love a nice creamy-beef-and-mushroom-saucey-kinda-thing with pasta? It its amongst the ranks of Steak and Three Veg as a real family raiser. A meal that's dolloped out after soccer, footy or netball training, by mum on a Thursday night. It's named after some Russian bloke Pavel or something, and apparently comes from Russia, but gee whiz we've made it our own, haven't we? It's rumoured that in the US of A, they serve the stuff up on rice occasionally, which sounds bloody awful, doesn't it? For all the families out there, Beef Strog is a solid dish, with a dash of 'exotic flavour', that does the job, time after time.

WHO DOESN'T LOVE A NICE CREAMY-BEEF-AND-MUSHROOM-SAUCEY-KINDA-THING WITH PASTA?

SEAFOOD

BEST SERVED WITH

Corona with a slice of lime

Seafood sauce

CUISINE STAPLES

Prawns from Thailand

Moreton Bay bugs

Saltwater yabbies

Fish fingers

BEST OCCASIONS

Christmas

Camping holidays

If you're ever craving something crisp, fresh and salty in Betoota, you may find yourself taking the risk and ordering the Fresh Seafood down at the Golf Club. Only available on Friday and Saturday nights, you can find yourself shucking oysters and shelling prawns like an inner-city socialite with this top-of-the-market option. However, for those of you who aren't based more than a thousand clicks from the coast, a Styrofoam box of prawns or a dozen oysters is more of a regular Aussie treat. It's a tradition for most families across this great country of ours to huddle around the table and shell a couple of kilos of prawns at Easter or Christmas. While dipping the tasty little pink crustaceans in seafood sauce you're bound to hear the phrase: 'Gee, these prawns are good, aren't they?' spouted from the mouths of at least three or four family members. They're right though, there isn't much better than wrangling open that white box of ice and seafood on a stinking hot Aussie afternoon and filling your gullet. In Australia, it's mandatory to indulge in Fish and Chips whenever you see a venue with plastic strip curtains and sand on the cream-white tile floor.

Best enjoyed by the sea, or if you feel the need to gamble needlessly with your life, then enjoy it as far away as Eromanga.

BEST SPOTS

1. Bluey's
~h and Chips in Broome

2. Ballina
Fishermen's
Co-Op

3. Andy's Fish
and Chip Shop in
Newcastle

PAVLOVA

BEST PLACE TO FIND IT

Beryl's house

Barbara's house

Ethyl's house

Marlene's house

Joan's house

BEST SERVED WITH

A cup of tea

Great family company

BEST OCCASIONS

Family birthdays
Sundays
Family gatherings

Prima ballerina of the early 1900s, Anna Pavlova is probably looking down in wonder and awe at the legacy she has left behind. The famous Russian dancer surely couldn't have known that she would be responsible for one of the greatest desserts the planet has ever seen and, more importantly a long-running feud between two countries so far from that of her birth. Our mouthy neighbours from across the 'dutch' will try and tell you that they created Pavlova, but it's nothing other than a great lie.

In this era of alternative facts and truths, they may try and carry it, but it's pretty commonly recognised by our grandparents that the Kiwi claim to pavlova is bullshit, just like their 2015 RWC win over us. I mean, it's referred to as a Great Aussie Dish. It's hard to imagine them cooking a pav in a hangi, isn't it? That aside, does it get any better than a sweet crunchy dessert topped with cream and fruit? If you actually asked yourself that question, no, it doesn't. The second-best thing your grandma has ever done, after giving you a

Like most things from New Zealand, Pavlova is crispy and tough on the outside, but overly gooey in the middle.

---

bloodline, is providing a constant stream of exceptional Pavlovas from birth. It's a real win for all involved. While you and your family members enjoy a scrumptious desert, Grandma will look around the table with a deep sense of satisfaction that can't be erased for at least an hour. Out in Western Queensland, we refer to it as the Betoota Birthday Cake.

CORNED BEEF

Vegetables

Any house in the suburbs

Tuesdays

Bread and cheese the next day

Any house in rural Australia

Smoko

Corned, or 'Bully', Beef is about as honest as your grandfather, who grew up in the Great Depression, fought in the war, worked 12 hour days all his life and never once pissed it away on grog, smokes or punting. It's a morsel born in a hardworking and modest time. Originally popular during the world wars, when meat was rationed, it's become its own acquired taste for a simple no-frills meal. While no Roast Lamb with Mint Sauce, it's a staple that has raised many Australian families and remains a soft spot for many. It was and still is especially popular in places like Betoota and throughout rural Australia, due to the preserving nature of salt. Ultimately, you'd never order it at a restaurant or even the Golf Club, but when you're old enough to understand its simple beauty, you'd never complain about it at home either.

WHILE NO ROAST LAMB WITH MINT SAUCE, IT'S A STAPLE THAT HAS RAISED MANY AUSTRALIAN FAMILIES AND REMAINS A SOFT SPOT FOR MANY.

WORKS BURGER

BEST SERVED WITH

Solo/Passiona

Chips/potato scallops drowned in chicken salt

MUST CONTAIN

Non-organic beetroot

Tinned pineapple

Sesame bun

Caged egg

BEST OCCASIONS

Hungover

When unsure what to do for dinner

On site

If you want to get a plain burger, go to McDonald's. If you want to get a real burger, go to your local café and order a 'Works Burger', with the lot. They have to ask, 'Would you like the lot?' when you order, but it's more of a formality than an actual question. You always have the lot. It would be like ordering Fish and Chips with no tartare sauce, or a Vietnamese roll with no chilli. It's incredible to think that there was a point in time when putting an egg and pineapple on a meat

IT'S INCREDIBLE TO THINK THAT THERE WAS A POINT IN TIME WHEN PUTTING AN EGG AND PINEAPPLE ON A MEAT SANDWICH WOULD HAVE SEEMED SO FOREIGN AND WEIRD.

sandwich would have seemed so foreign and weird. It's a suitable meal for any point in the day. Whether you're moseying around at 7 p.m., wondering what the bloody hell you should have for dinner, or you've just dug a trench on site and are outrageously hungry, the Works Burger is for you. Wondering how you're going to fit that first bite in your mouth, and having the greasy juices run down your fingers and hands, is the Works Burger experience. You simply can't be critical of it.

BEST SPOTS

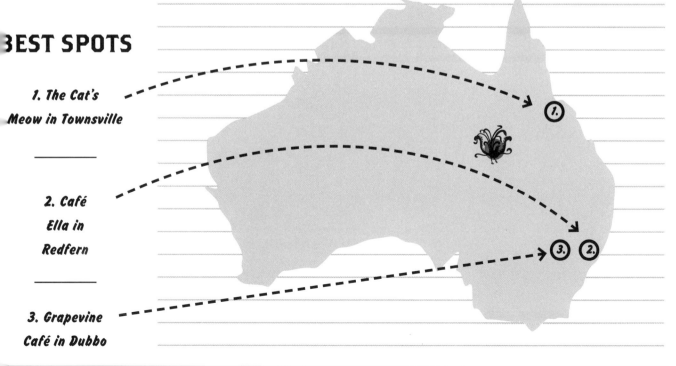

1. The Cat's
Meow in Townsville

———

2. Café
Ella in
Redfern

———

3. Grapevine
Café in Dubbo

SPAG BOL

BEST PLACE TO FIND IT

Any Australian family household at the end of the pay packet

Any sharehouse at the start of the pay packet

BEST SERVED WITH

*Parmesan cheese
Tasty cheese (if no parmesan available)
Mozarella cheese (if none of the above are available)*

BEST OCCASIONS

The last night of a family reunion

The first night your boyfriend cooks you dinner

Much like the appropriation of Asian butter chicken and sweet and sour pork, Italian food has also been Australianised and deconstructed into a meal that does not require too much worldliness in kitchens around the country.

Spag Bol, sometimes referred to as Spag Bog, is one of the most warming, homely meals in the country. Its name is derived from the Italian-Australian specialty of Spaghetti Bolognese.

Minced beef, tomatoes, cheese, carrots and onion can be used to make thousands of non-Oriental meals, but when combined with pasta, it becomes something that makes all walks of Australians pinch

OFTEN UNDERSOLD BY AUSTRALIAN MUMS.

their fingers together and say words like 'bellissimo' and 'al dente'.

While most real Italians would argue that it's a complete bastardisation of one of their less glamorous household staples, it is also recognised as one of the reasons that Australians have gradually pushed the boat out to other ethnic meals – like Pesto Pasta and Fettucine Carbonara.

While universally loved by children coming home late from school sports, it is often undersold by Australian mums, who refer to it as 'just a spag bol'.

A staple in every household, from the most hopeless, unattractive bachelor to the homes of the rich and famous, this is the omnipresent dish.

NOW HIRING

E.H. Pearson Pastoral Company
Betoota QLD

BET

THE S

AUS

THE CODES

The cricket bat and rugby ball are mightier than the pen and sword combined.

AUSTRALIAN FAVOURITES

Rugby League

Rugby Union

Victorian Football

Cricket

Soccer

Motorsport

Golf

The Rest

The Betoota Dolphins seen here in their 1967 Grand Final victory against the Windorah Jellyfish.

IN ACCORDANCE WITH THE GAME'S BY-LAWS: 'THERE ARE TWELVE (12) PUBLIC SCANDALS THAT THE CLUB MUST ENDURE PUBLICLY PER ANNUM.'

Many of the local sports one might be familiar with in the Betoota region are also played in other areas of the country. The town's sporting teams are the lifeblood and fabric of society here – all except rugby union, which you can only play if you meet a stringent list of qualifying criteria.

Our grade cricketers don't differ much from the ones you'd find in the rest of the country. The club is an outlet for middle-class homeowners desperately chasing the glory they felt after their first and only century one wet Saturday morning in grade 11. The social atmosphere is hardly electric, but they're a good crowd to be around if you want to learn more about the Waugh-Warne era of Australian cricket.

The Betoota Dolphins rugby league team functions in a similar fashion to most other league sides. The team is funded in part by grants from governing bodies and in part by the money the townsfolk feed through the pokies down at the Dolphins Workies.

In accordance with the game's by-laws: 'there are twelve (12) public scandals that the club must endure publicly per annum, from domestic and public assaults, to drug convictions and drink-driving arrests, each scandal must be unique – but wholly detrimental to the code on the whole.'

On the other hand, the rugby union team, simply referred to as the rugby union team, expect a much higher standard from their players and club members. Their clubhouse has a dress code and the bar staff follow Responsible Service of Alcohol legislation stringently. As there is no private school of note in Betoota, they have imported players from the plains of Western Queensland to make up a team. A concept not lost on a lot of inner-city private schools, where the union gentlemen typically come from.

As for Victorian Football, our town is not a very good portfolio for the game. However, if you were to travel 400 kilometres west, into the Territory, you might be able to find a couple of fairly talented black kids kicking a Sherrin – or more conveniently, you could travel 200 kilometres south in the Free-settler Zone.

RUGBY LEAGUE

THE GREATEST
GAME OF ALL

'There are no great men – only great challenges, which ordinary men are forced by circumstances to meet.' – Wayne Bennett

As most Betoota residents know, rugby league has been a sports staple on the Eastern Seaboard since the Northern English brought it over in the early days of colonisation.

It's the game that has brought us some of our most iconic working-class heroes – Tommy Raudonikis, John Hopoate, Sam Thaiday – a mix of backgrounds and phrenetics truly uniting a community by the hollow clap of a shoulder going into a throat.

Since its inception, it seems almost like nothing can dint rugby league's popularity. No amount of drug scandals, sexual assault cases, drink-driving charges, dog-rooting videos or clandestine meetings with bookmakers can affect its standing.

For the layman, it is important to note that there are two codes of the game. There is rugby league, which is played in most reasonably sized towns and cities across the country, as well as professionally in the NRL. Then there is 'Bush League', which is played out Betoota way. These are two completely different games and the latter is often used as a form of rehab for those who get lost in the big smoke.

Bush League is considered hard and tough, but ultimately sensible when it

comes to on-field violence. Whereas the brand you see in Logan, Penrith or Blacktown can best be described as a 'bit more grubby'.

Down there, an on-field brawl can easily spew into a few blokes getting their heads kicked in out in the car park after the match. Out in the sticks, a punch-on usually doesn't

associated with the Great Game – some new, some old and some very detrimental to the fabric of society. But the game can always sit on its high horse when it comes to politics.

For one, unlike in our Southern codes, blackfellas don't get booed in the NRL – this is because league players themselves are considered

the NRL is also able to claim the first openly gay professional footballer in the world.

Ian 'The Most Violent Man in League' Roberts – who played for Manly, South Sydney and North Queensland in the '90s – was far too scary to call a 'poof'. The NRL has been a big supporter of gay rights ever since Manly versus Balmain, 1991, when Gary Jack was put in hospital.

As *The Daily Telegraph* also loves pointing out, on a professional level, the game has more links to organised crime than Frank Sinatra. This seedy underside has become part and parcel with NRL. You just need to look at the headlines on a monthly basis to see another professional player linked to some outlawed Bikie Gang.

NO AMOUNT OF DRUG SCANDALS, SEXUAL ASSAULT CASES, DRINK-DRIVING CHARGES, DOG-ROOTING VIDEOS OR CLANDESTINE MEETINGS WITH BOOKMAKERS CAN AFFECT ITS STANDING.

escalate beyond a sickening king-hit from a third-man-in. It's not exactly Queensberry Rules, but it's all fair in love and war, as they say.

There are a lot of stereotypes

to be second-class citizens and, like in the military, there is no room for elitism.

Another surprising phenomenon is the game's stance on LGBTI rights, as

Tattoos used to be a dead giveaway, in regards to which player knew ☞

THERE ARE A LOT OF STEREOTYPES ASSOCIATED WITH THE GREAT GAME – SOME NEW, SOME OLD AND SOME VERY DETRIMENTAL TO THE FABRIC OF SOCIETY.

a bloke from the Hell's Angels, but the game has changed. Gone are the days when only one-season-wonders would be rocking a spider-web on the elbow, or a quote in Latin across the throat. Now even the sweethearts, like Mitchell Pearce, are rocking a full sleeve. It's also a little bit harder to pick when clubs are employing criminals to run supplement programs.

But aside from the blow-ins and bad influences, the game has always been built around community – and the true community comes from the 'stayers' – the volunteers, the old codgers and the matriarchal canteen mums. Everyone knows if there were a few more women named 'Deb' getting around the NRL, there'd be a lot more fear and sensibility put into the players.

A recent study conducted by the NRL concluded that only 3 per cent of players can run without their head.

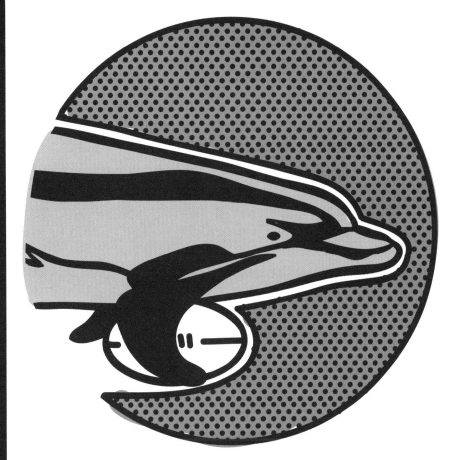

CCRL PREMIERS 1967

THE MIGHTY

BETOOTA DOLPHINS

— RUGBY LEAGUE FC —

RUGBY UNION

THE GAME THEY
PLAY IN HEAVEN

'In 1823, William Webb Ellis first picked up the ball in his arms and ran with it. And for the next 156 years forwards have been trying to work out why.' – Sir Tasker Watkins (1979)

Rugby union. It's a game steeped in nostalgia and tradition. The game they play in heaven. The mighty Wallabies. John Eales, the Ella Brothers, Stirling Mortlock and his stupid bloody gloves – and now Charlotte Caslick and the Aussie Sevens.

No one has forgotten what it was like when we'd win Bledisloes – the baggy green-and-gold jerseys, worn by amateur-looking blokes trying to cut through the Kiwi or Saffa line. Out in Betoota, a few of the old boys still love the game. Blokes who grew up in an era when everyone seemed to care about the Wallabies. When you didn't have to pay tens of thousands of dollars to go to an elite private school to get a start.

Yes, it was always more of an upper-class game, but it was something we could all get behind – when John Williamson would pull out the guitar and sing 'Waltzing Matilda' in rebuttal to the haka.

From a young age, most Australian Rugby Union (ARU) players will note that it's the Polynesian lads who are feeding flair back into the game. The physically superior, happy-go-lucky players – whose ancestry often stems from Samoa, Fiji or Tonga – are renowned for their high-pitched giggles and outrageous offloads – as well as their cultural ties to New Zealand, the Rugby Capital of the World.

The Kiwi contribution to Rugby culture, on and off the field, is highly valued in suburban clubland. The game wouldn't be half of what it is today without the Islander influence – in fact it would look like a lot more like a Young Liberals function.

The formula of building teams from working-class FOBs from the backblocks of south Auckland alongside gym-junkie private schoolers is one that exists right across the country. From the blueblood bush union clubs in the North to the Range Rover–bordered ovals of Sydney, this formula is found in a number of Kiwi-populated Southern holdouts across Melbourne, Perth and Adelaide – even Hobart.

The blond-haired GPS School superstar with a jumper tied across his shoulders is a well-recognised stereotype for the game. It's the man who believes he was cut from a better stone and turns up to Game Day sporting a pair of R.M. Williams boots and cream-coloured chinos – the true Concrete Cowboy with a stranglehold on ARU.

He'll only outgrow the stereotype when he becomes an 'Old Boy' – at which point he'll become completely versed in the scrums and backline moves of his son's u9s side, and will spend his weekends yelling: 'Stop. Kicking. The Bloody Ball away,' from the sidelines in every game.

Rugby union in contemporary Australia, although well funded, is lacking many prospects outside the dual-coding Polynesian and Aboriginal players, as the game is carried by the sons of stockbrokers fresh from the GPS competition.

However, one positive to come from the unfortunate state of our Super Rugby competition is the support that has been redirected to our female rugby union players, who have been winning enough matches to get the whole country behind them, as well as an Olympic gold medal.

FROM THE BLUEBLOOD BUSH UNION CLUBS IN THE NORTH TO THE RANGE ROVER–BORDERED OVALS OF SYDNEY ...

VICTORIAN FOOTBALL

THE GAME

THEY PLAY IN VICTORIA AND SOME OTHER PLACES

'The Game Victorians Play in Heaven'

Although Betoota's proximity to South Australia should dictate a love of Victorian Football, it has never taken off in the area.

Victorian Football can be described as 'one hell of a spectator sport'. That is, if you are watching it at the MCG. Unfortunately for advertisers, the game doesn't translate well to a television screen. This may well be the reason that the game hasn't taken off in the Australian Pacific North-East – as the further you travel from Melbourne, the less likely you will be to experience a high-quality match in person.

It's popular with the Aboriginal Australian community in the deep West, as well as with the hip Millennial youth, who've turn their backs on the more colonial codes of football.

However, not a whole lot is known about Victorian Rules in Betoota, as the only representative team the town produced defected to South Yarra during a tour of Melbourne in 1992. Nonetheless, a small number of Southern expats maintain a small club with the help of local government grants, which has grown to be the perennial easy-beats of the Diamantina Victorian Rules Championship.

THE ONLY REPRESENTATIVE TEAM BETOOTA PRODUCED DEFECTED TO SOUTH YARRA.

Some players run up to 30km in a single game of football. Others also run around.

Played on the Leonard Avenue Oval over the dry season, which could be any time between February and November, only one 'first-grade' team competes in the local third-grade competition.

So dire is their ability to function as a club, the team song is rumoured to be 'Take Me Out' by Scottish pop-rock band Franz Ferdinand.

With that said, support for the fledgling side is growing around the town. But many still feel that it's a bridge too far to get behind a VFL team.

One casual observer remarked that it looks like a game with many rules, while appearing to have no rules at all. One thing everyone can agree on is the athletic ability needed to play the game at an elite level – which it isn't in Betoota. There is nothing elite about Victorian Rules in Betoota.

CRICKET

THE GENTLEMAN'S GAME

'They came to see me bat not you bowl!' W.G. Grace said, putting the bails back on his stumps after getting bowled.

Aptly named the 'gentleman's game', the physical and mental marathon that is the sport of cricket rightly sits atop the cultural pyramid of Betootanese society.

It is important for a cricketer to have a sense of humour; not essential, but it almost always helps. Because like life in the Diamantina, cricket doesn't always go your way – but when it does, there's nothing better.

The game has and always will be popular in our area, which is often the case, as you'll discover on your travels around this Great Land.

Players are divided into grades and pitted against one another in the nets.

Cricket does not bear the sharp socioeconomic edges of the town's football codes; it is life's great level battleground. Where even the most spoon-fed Protestant private schoolboy can build a partnership with any man, woman or child born less well-off – as well as spend an afternoon ducking and diving from their right-arm around-the-wicket.

The game is popular because we're good at it. That is the Australian way.

While the more popular sports such as European football and the lesser ball games enjoy unbridled growth, like a disinterested stepfather, they'll never be an apt replacement for the real thing – which is cricket.

The three grade and one youth teams that you see train each Tuesday and Thursday at the Leonard Avenue Oval are giants of the competition. But you probably already knew that.

Because it takes two pubs and a police station to support a rugby league team, but it takes an entire town to keep a cricket side afloat.

From Ludwig Remienko, curator of the Leonard Avenue Oval, to Hershel de Villiers, the opening first-grade batsman – if Betoota didn't hold the game they actually play in heaven up on such a pedestal, it'd suffer the same fate that Victorian Football did.

However, while a certain amount of local prestige is one thing, not everyone has the required hand-eye coordination to enjoy the game at a socially acceptable level. For that, we

The Sydney Cricket Ground is a melting pot of cultures, creeds, mid-strength beer and a pure love of a game that ties that all together. Sport also happens there.

have the seasonal sport of swimming (if you can even call it a sport).

Cricket doesn't stare down her long, elegant nose at those who can't wrap their heads around her complexities and character; she embraces them and welcomes them into the fray.

For those who love the game, but cannot play it, there are a number of supporting roles that one can play to aid those who can – and will – play the game.

THE CLUBMAN

Like a true leader of men, the Clubman is the first to put foot on the oval on a Saturday morning and is often the last to walk off it. Without the Clubman, there is no Club. But the Clubman doesn't play the game anymore, he or she gave it up years ago. An injury perhaps. Quite often, age has wearied their bodies

to a point where copping a short one would simply kill them. But they keep the memories of their youth close at hand. Quick to offer advice to the next nervous man in. Seen observing the youngsters trying to roll one out of the back of their hand behind the tuckshop, only to step in to explain that the ring finger makes or breaks a good right-armed leg spin.

The Clubman's love for the game is both inspiring and intimidating. Why do you even bother playing the game, you ask yourself as you walk back to the sheds, moments after being clean bowled for six. The Clubman

is standing beside the gate with a smile on his face, telling you not to worry. Just like he stands, when you're walking off the ground ahead of the captain after taking five quick ones to win the game an over before stumps.

MR ALL THE GEAR AND NO IDEA

Despite averaging slightly better than Courtney Walsh did on an international level, the seventh-drop specialist batsman, striding to the crease with a $900 bat under his arm, isn't as rare as you'd think.

They own every bit of cricket kit and tool on the market. Looking to change the grip on your bat? Look no further than this man. Not only will he have whatever you call the cone thing you use to roll them on, he'll even do it for you. Because, like the Clubman, he loves the game and he plays it for love only.

If he's coming in to face a savage pace attack, this man will look like RoboCop. There won't be a silverside of flesh left naked to feel the sting of red leather.

Should your innings depend on the tail wagging, do not depend on this person. They will take the piss liberally. Facing only their second ball when they spot something on a good length outside off? You bet they're going to have a go at slapping it over cover. Sometimes they'll get four for their risk, other times they'll chop it onto the stumps or spoon it to cover itself. Do not depend on the person will all the gear, unless it's for help tightening the spikes on your boots.

Most players enjoy a love–hate relationship with this person, like George Harrison and Eric Clapton had with each other.

But, like the Clubman, the Club would fall to bits without the bloke who owns half the team kit anyway.

SOCCER

THE
WORLD GAME

'I think this is my favourite type of rugby' – Malcolm Turnbull

Soccer, or Football as some call it, has taken a bit of a hold on the younger generations in South-Western Queensland. Much like the rest of Australia, the 'World Game' has risen sharply in popularity in and around the Shire of Diamantina. Initially only spoken about in garages owned by immigrants from Europe, soccer has now spread into many Anglo households – with a growing tribe of middle-class mums now choosing Soccer for their kids as an alternative to concussions and broken arms.

Often described as 'wogball' or 'pooftahball' – as coined by the late great Socceroo Johnny Warren – the game has grown rapidly across Australia since one of the Spice Girls married David Beckham. While there are still some purists who reckon the game is too soft, a couple of World Cup appearances have meant that the game's popularity has even reached rural Australia and the Top End. Even though the national A-League competition may not be of a great standard when compared to English Premier League, and the concept of 'diving' for penalties can upset the bloodthirsty Australian punter, the unruly behaviour of flare-waving crowds in Western Sydney is enough to earn the respect of most of our nation's young men and women with authority complexes. But without a doubt, the current success seen by 'foooootbowllll' in this country comes down to the persistence and financial aid of the Post-war Wog – the Frank Lowys of this country, who built clubs out of council parks and made Socceroos out of their sons. While Les Murray and Johnny Warren became the faces of Soccer in Australia, it's the continental Mums and Dads who built it.

If you stacked the ASIO files of every attendee at an A-League game on top of each other, it would be very tall and unstable.

OFTEN DESCRIBED AS 'WOGBALL' OR 'POOFTAHBALL'.

MOTORSPORT

THE GENTLEMAN'S SHAME

**'Finishing races is important, but racing is more important.'
— Dale Earnhardt**

If rugby union is the game they play in heaven and cricket is a sport for gentlemen, then Australian motorsport is the game they play on earth and the sport played by men.

Unapologetically loud and fast, the fans of Australian motorsport are often the most vocal, tribal and passionate. The vehicles on the other hand are among the fastest four-door racers on the planet. Home to a Formula One event, home to our own brand of go-fast motoring and home to world champions in all forms of the game, Australia's dedication to motorsport is unwavering.

In saying that, there's a number of things that make Australian motorsport different from any other sport in the country.

It's very popular and those who do it, love it. That's something that puts them at odds with the everyday Australian, who can only admit to a casual interest in any form of sport. Sport is a periphery in the lives of the majority, but not with those who have racing fuel coursing through their veins. Because of this, many of the self-described cultural elite consider motorsport fans to be some sort of mouth-breathing cretins with a lust for speed and an unquenchable thirst for bottom shelf spirits.

While it's abhorrent to judge a man, or woman, on their interests and pursuits outside of their mindless job, the case for the motorsport enthusiast isn't helped by home truths such as the V8 Supercars limiting the amount of alcohol one can bring into an event to one carton per person per day. Other examples of this include the divide between General Motors and Ford, despite both come from the same suburb in Detroit.

It's also shocking to most well-adjusted people that a person would get a tattoo of their respective racing team somewhere permanently visible, such as the neck, throat or back of hand. Most fan clubs make that a requirement to join.

A wise man once said, however,

Above/Left: Grid girls and crashes are the greatest draw cards in motor sport.

that it's the fans that make the sport. For all the flak the media and social climbers give motorsport fans, they keep bouncing back. This is most evident at the annual Bathurst 1000, the everyman's playground. For a week, tens of thousands of Supercars fans descend on the sleeping mid-western gateway town of Bathurst for four days of baking sun, sexless drinking and common assault.

Perhaps that's what gives the sport a bad name in the boring bourgeoisie circles of communal autofellatio and self-important ego pumping that is the professional class. Perhaps it's something else. The only solid advice that can be given when dealing with Australian motorsport is to be prepared for anything – as you're probably going to see it.

IT'S SHOCKING TO MOST WELL-ADJUSTED PEOPLE THAT A PERSON WOULD GET A TATTOO OF THEIR RESPECTIVE RACING TEAM SOMEWHERE PERMANENTLY VISIBLE, SUCH AS THE NECK, THROAT OR BACK OF HAND.

GOLF

THE GAME THEY PLAY BEFORE HEAVEN

'Achievements on the golf course are not what matters, decency and honesty are what matter' – Tiger Woods

It takes a rare breed of human to enjoy a game of golf, let alone watch one. Not only does it take the patience of ten men, it also takes the wallet of five. It tests the mental resolve of even the most seasoned and calm individual – and people wonder why every surgeon in the country owns a set of golf clubs.

Which leads to the inevitability of running into a doctor on the course or being paired with one. That's another thing about golfing. If you're the only one in your circle of mates who enjoys a game, you either end up throwing your clubs in the creek or you have to play with strangers.

Playing golf with strangers means you can't cheat with impunity, which goes against the spirit of the game. Not cheating in golf is heavily frowned upon, especially when playing with lawyers and those who work in finance.

Be that as it may, close to all the members at the exclusive Royal Betoota Golf Club work in the industries mentioned before, which may or may not turn you off the idea of ever picking up a club. However, there are honest and pleasant people who play golf socially.

Those people are the elderly. The

golf course is the pleasuredome of the aged and weary, their Kubla Khan, their Xanadu. Playing the back nine can leave the most athletic young man feeling sore the next day – imagine how an 80-year-old retired insurance broker would feel after a slow and steady 18. The most senior members of the golfing community are the true ambassadors for the sport, not the chinless Audi-driving portfolio managers in their polo shirts.

Nevertheless, there is some merit to having some tangible golfing ability. A countless number of business deals have been done on golf courses. It's where professional men and women come to separate the wheat from the executive chaff. A game of golf can be so much more than just a game of golf. As mentioned before, it's a game that tests your mind and body like no other. Unlike cricket, you don't have a team of mates cheering you on in support. It's just you, the club and the ball. Add the pressure of having someone directly involved with the progress of your career watching you hit the thing – it can get a bit too much.

But if you pull it off, you'll enjoy all the fruits of a long career doing exactly what you're told.

Playing golf with strangers means you can't cheat with impunity, which goes against the spirit of the game.

Royal Betoota Golf Club is one of the oldest and most exclusive clubs in the wider Diamantina area. Some say Sir Joh buried eighteen of his worst enemies under each green.

THE REST

OTHER

AUSTRALIAN SPORTS

'The greatest honour any Australian swimmer can get is having a ferry named after you. I'm still waiting.' — Geoff Huegill

Aside from the winter footballs, cricket and horseracing, it would seem that Australians seldom give a shit about many other sports. This is not the case.

One of the great, unsung codes of Australian sport, funnily enough, belongs to our sisters and daughters. They are supreme athletes, and the sport continues to grow without the funding, headlines or sensationalism of other male-dominated codes.

Like the iceberg that sank the Titanic, the majority of Australian Netball exists under the surface and out of sight. It's an undeniable dark horse of daytime TV, broadcast solely for the living rooms of suburban mums with faint scars on their knees

from past injuries on the court.

Since 1995, netball has been a recognised Olympic sport, which has helped dramatically with their grassroots efforts – Australians will always back anything that could result in Gold.

It is for this reason that swimming is considered to be one of our country's most popular sports, once every four years.

Australia's habit of breaking world records – and of forcing young men and women to spend the best years of their lives face down in wet, lonely silence – has pushed swimming to front of the fray when it comes to international competition.

With names like Hackett, Leisel,

Rice, Huegill, Madam Butterfly, Klim and the Thorpedo – our Gestapo-style junior swimming programs have ensured that we flog the best out of our water-based athletes while they are young.

Unfortunately, like a lot of our disposable household names, Swimming has also become known for monumental fuck-ups, which our medal-winners often endure post-retirement.

Be it with cocaine, fast food, prescription drugs, offensive tweets or nipple cripples – it is now very clear that the Olympic flame burns twice as bright, for half as long.

However, aside from swimming, not all of our eligible Olympians

SWIMMING HAS ALSO BECOME KNOWN FOR MONUMENTAL FUCK-UPS.

Right: Swimming is great for the body and soul. That's if you like being alone with your thoughts staring at a line.

really give too much of a fuck about gold medals – especially when they can make twenty times more money in more frequent competitions. Sports like golf and tennis are often lacking in talent, with the young fellas opting to make the most out of their careers in non-Government-funded tours.

With or without the Olympics, when it comes to golf, we hit and miss. The rise of the sport in Asia has seen our standards slip. Greg Norman's 40-year reign is now a faint memory, as the Chinese, Thai and Korean talent pool grows bigger than our entire AIS.

Tennis, however, is still something we can hold onto with pride – despite the fact that the behaviour of our best players is not often something we can be proud of. Much like golf and spelling bees, tennis is a game held up by overly competitive parents and bratty kids.

If memory serves correctly, our tennis brats go through phases – starting as brats but ending up quite likeable. Philippoussis and Lleyton did it, so we all have fingers crossed for Kyrgios and Tomic. Come on boys!!!

BET

LANG

AUS

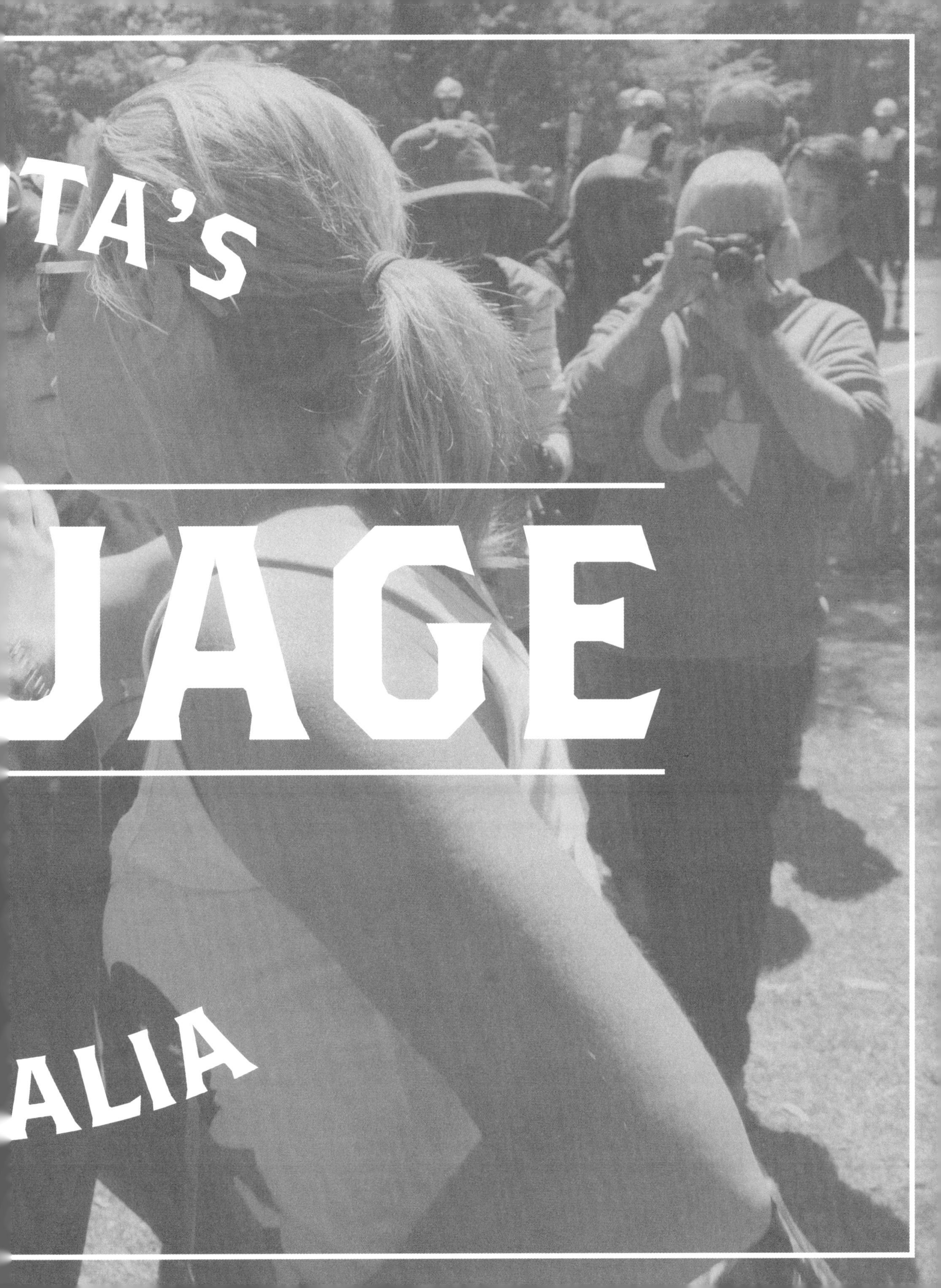
TA'S
UAGE
ALIA

AUSTRALIAN DIALECTS

'Never complain; never explain' – Kerry Packer's personal motto

LANGUAGE GROUPS

Interior Australian English

Received Australian

Standard Woglish

Australian Aboriginal English (Blackfella)

The Perth Accent

The Melbourne Acc'nt

Free Settler English

Betootan Pidgin

To the layperson, each Australian – no matter their class, education or colour – speaks with the same tongue.

We all sound the same.

While you may be able to select 'Australian English' when setting up your phone, or tell a computer you still like seeing 'colour' with a 'u', the fact of the matter is that there are many different dialects, accents and languages flourishing across Australia that often go unnoticed.

Some are geographical, others cultural, and some are both those things. However, it's important to remember that the dialects, languages and accents mentioned in this guide only represent a small sliver of what's actually out there.

Take our own language, Betootanese Pidgin. Found almost nowhere else in the country, but in our region, it's the first language in 90 per cent of households. In the wider South-West, it's the second language of close to half the population, with Standard Interior as the mother tongue for most.

Other geographical accents, such as the Melbourne, Perth and Free Settler, are as unique and far apart idiomatically as they are geographically.

Those speaking the warm and friendly Free Settler accent choose to not mince their words, but to pensively project each syllable into a room with the confidence of a disgraced politician who refuses to resign.

Arguably the most isolated of our accents, the Perth or West Coast dialect is the most adaptable and easiest to understand. The city on the Swan was built on the back of domestic migration last century, so the way they speak in the West is a mélange of the entire nation.

Stoked by the flames of culture,

TAKE OUR OWN LANGUAGE, BETOOTANESE PIDGIN. FOUND ALMOST NOWHERE ELSE IN THE COUNTRY BUT IN OUR REGION, IT'S THE FIRST LANGUAGE IN 90 PER CENT OF HOUSEHOLDS.

Above: The Bilpa Morea Stone. Engraved in it is the original Betootan Pidgin dictionary.

Australian Aboriginal English is a language caught between two worlds. Like the others, it creates identity and a sense of belonging – which is something we all want and deserve.

Be sure to read through these guides; you'll quickly learn to speak the way they do beyond the dunes.

INTERIOR AUSTRALIAN ENGLISH

Never rushed, never wasted, spoken with purpose, poise and persistence, interior Australian English is our national voice of reason, the one you follow in a crisis. The dialect bleeds from the bush.

Spoken slowly but often said twice, Interior Australian English [IAE] was born out of isolation, an honest day's work and knowing when to say when.

Often described as the most pensive and thoughtful of all Australian dialects, it's easy to identify when you hear it. Made up exclusively of long pauses, drawn-out and hyper-stressed vowels, as well as your run-of-the-mill sociolinguistic gymnastics, the dialect is among the rarest you'd hear in cosmopolitan Australia. It can be difficult to understand at times, but is universally respected.

However, that hasn't stopped many big city 'entertainers' and 'actors' from trying to lampoon the Interior accent for the enjoyment of their inner-city peers. From Paul Hogan to that bloke from *Kath & Kim*, many have tried and many have failed to capture the quiet, polite, sanguine timbre that a person of the hot country speaks with. It's a voice with timing and purpose, which often lends itself to storytelling and the odd long-winded joke.

Warming his hands against the campfire in his front yard, local pastoralist Jack Pearson said he's often asked where he's from, whenever he leaves the district for a busier place.

'Yeah look, mate,' he said before a brief pause. 'You can tell a lot about a bloke by keeping your mouth shut.

Pictured: The Hon. Bob Katter, Member For Kennedy [centre]
Clancy Overell [left] speak in the Interior Australian Dialect, while
Errol Parker [right] does his best to hide his Received Accent.

I mean, you can listen to some bloke jibber on about God-knows-what for an hour and still not know what he's talking about. You're only worth as much as your word out here in the bush, so we tend to pick our words carefully. You know what I'm talking about, joog?'

While most ethnic Betootanese people speak IAE as a second language, researchers have observed a merging of the two to form an unofficial hybrid dialect, similar to

the 'Spanglish' phenomenon in the United States and Mexico.

Often seen after a number of drinks, some of the longer pauses seen in the Interior accent after often made shorter and filler words, which are almost non-existent in the language, are noticeably present.

These filler words which can be heard in inner-city dialects – words such as 'um', 'uh', 'er', 'ah', 'like', 'okay', 'right' and 'you know' – are replaced with a swear word.

For example, if you were to ask an IAE speaker if they got any rain in the last lot, a sober morning conversation wouldn't stray much further than: 'Nah, nah, not this time, mate,' whereas one at a quarter past nine at a weekend rodeo would be much more colourful. Something along the lines of: 'Nah, mate. I'm having a c—t of a time out there, you know. A real c—t of a time. The bank manager and I really needed a drop.'

RECEIVED
AUSTRALIAN
PRONUNCIATION

From the deepest darkest corner of Toorak to the tallest Queenslanders of Ascot, the Received Australian stands as a beacon of wealth, power and the complete detachment from everyday society.

Often confused with the similar, but equally charming Melbourne and Free Settler accents, Received Pronunciation often gets a bad rap. This is because it's more than just a particular way somebody speaks; it's a way of life. Almost all Australians who speak with the Received accent don't work with their hands – they use their minds, thoughts and astute enunciation to stride effortlessly through social engagements that any normal person would dive under a coal train to avoid.

A 2001 study, conducted by a South Betoota TAFE student, was able to establish a link between the dead-fish handshake and Received Pronunciation. This finding was backed up by Betoota Mayor, Councillor Keith Carton. After shaking hands with the then Governor of Queensland, Quentin Bryce (pictured, opposite), he remarked that her handshake was 'piss-weak'.

Nonetheless, these are the Australians who are running the nation – for richer and poorer – but if a child of a single parent from deepest darkest inner-western Sydney can rise up to be Prime Minister, then you too can learn how to speak like Cate Blanchett.

For more than forty years, Gwendolyn Maxwell has been running elocution classes for the town's youth lucky enough to win a place at university. From a small room in the North Betoota PCYC, she's taught generations how to speak, act and react when in the company of the inner-city elite, which is a situation a countless number of young, well-to-do country folk have found themselves in before.

'The first thing I teach is to speak with your mouth open. There's not many flies down in the city, so you don't have to speak through the side of your mouth,' she said. 'Then we move on to completing words, instead of merely replacing your Gs

with apostrophes. For words that end in a sharp consonant, I insist that you must vocalise it.'

Aside from propping up more than one struggling South American economy, those with this blessed accent can also rely on their connections to help them find their place. Chances are, if you know a person who enjoys saying France, Dance and Chance with impunity, you've met a person who's come from an embarrassingly high-net-worth family.

A 2001 STUDY CONDUCTED BY A BUDDING BETOOTA THESP STUDENT WAS ABLE TO ESTABLISH A LINK BETWEEN THE DEAD-FISH HANDSHAKE AND DECEIVED PRONUNCIATION.

STANDARD WOGLISH

Though it's a relatively new language in comparison to some of the others, Standard Woglish has flourished and spread as far and wide as those who brought it to our shores many, many moons ago.

While not strictly a language unto itself, Standard Woglish is arguably the most recognisable and distinctive of all Australian English dialects. Falling into a number of subcategories, this unique dialect is often restricted to the more cosmopolitan areas of the nation, such as capital cities and soccer matches.

Spoken by the nation's first and second wave of Mediterranean and Middle Eastern immigrants, the accent has woven itself into the fabric of the nation, but it has undergone its own trials and tribulations. Ethnically Lebanese, Greek, Italian, Palestinian and other parts of the world are the primary speakers of Standard Woglish. But what sets them apart from one another is how their mother tongue has spliced itself into their everyday interpretation of Australian English.

Famous speakers of Standard Woglish include Greek-Australian actors Nick Giannopoulos and Vincenzo Colosimo, who are arguably the trailblazers of the dialect, as well as Lebanese-Australian underworld figures such as The Hon. Bob Katter and John Ibrahim and various sportsmen from Beau Ryan to Hazem El Masri.

A standard continental Australian home complete with fibreglass pillars.

Locally, there are four registered Standard Woglish speakers in the greater Betoota area, according to census data. Daroo Used & New Vehicles owner, Victorian-born Greek businessman Constance Georgiou, speaks in a strong Woglish accent and has been serving the community in Betoota for over two decades. In his own words: Standard Woglish.

Right: World Champion boxer Jeff Fenech was instrumental in bringing Standard Woglish into the everyday vernacular of Australians and people around the world.

'I LOVE YOUSE ALL.'

AUSTRALIAN ABORIGINAL ENGLISH

A language intertwined and sandwiched between two worlds, Australian Aboriginal English takes the oldest of dialects and voices from the country and blends it with a voice of the new world.

NOTABLE SPEAKERS

David Gulpilil

Eddie Mabo

Charles Perkins

Ernie Dingo

Nova Peris

Noel Pearson

Anthony Mundine

AREAS

The Top End

Everywhere

Aboriginal English, known also as Australian Aboriginal English or Blackfella English, is a dialect of Australian English used by a large section of the Indigenous Australian population.

It varies greatly from region to region, with some accents being thicker than others. However, the fundamentals remain the same. Speakers have been noted to change between different forms of the language, depending on who they are speaking to: for example, when speaking to a Migloo.

— 'WE ARE WORKING OUT HERE IN THE SUN AND IT'S STINKING HOT.'

Similar to 'Spanglish' – a hybrid language observed in parts of Southern California – Australian Aboriginal English substitutes Indigenous words and slang for English in sentences.

Aboriginal English does not use unnecessary words. For example, the Aboriginal English equivalent of: 'We are working out here in the sun and it's stinking hot,' would be: 'We workin' and it's stinkin'.' Linguistics researchers don't regard this as 'just dropping words out', but as a language unto itself.

Another interesting aspect of this dialect, as you probably already know, is the social and cultural underpinning that gave birth to it in the first place. Using family terms, such as uncle, father, sister, brother and so on, are applicable not just to one's immediate family, but to anyone in the community of the appropriate age.

Nevertheless, it's the only Australian dialect to have a background rooted in culture. The others are merely born out of isolation and education level. This alone makes Aboriginal English one of the most important cultural aspects of Australia.

THE
PERTH
ACCENT

Undeniably palatable, with pangs of the somewhat abrasive South African accent that makes the roughest cat's tongue seem silky, the Perth Accent is versatile and multicultural, a phenomenon that could only happen in the world's most isolated city.

AREAS

Fremantle

Peppermint Grove

Coogee Beach (Perth)

Around the Swan River

Bunbury

Everywhere in between

It's a common misconception that the Perth Accent is similar to the Melbourne, Free Settler and Received Pronunciation accents, but it's not. People from Perth who speak like that just went to private school.

The honest-and-true Perth accent borrows from every dialect in the country. It is the bubble and squeak of accents. Owing to its isolation, not only from the rest of Australia but the rest of the world, the Perth accent is one of the strangest ways to speak and understand English.

Try to imagine somebody with a strong Melbourne Acc'nt imitating someone from Sydney, but overdoing it. It slips in and out – from sounding rough and abrasive to astute and round – at the drop of a hat.

While some of the other accents and dialects mentioned in this guide may be difficult for a young Betootan to understand at first, the Perth Accent shouldn't cause you any trouble. It's slow and friendly enough for even the coyest cowboy to understand and converse with.

However, despite the recent population growth in Western Australia, the Perth accent is beginning to die out.

Fly-in-fly-out workers are being blamed for polluting the pristine linguistic environment that's existed on the West Coast for countless generations. Their East Coast twang and boring, lazy pronunciation of

FLY-IN-FLY-OUT WORKERS ARE BEING BLAMED FOR POLLUTING THE PRISTINE LINGUISTIC ENVIRONMENT THAT'S EXISTED ON THE WEST COAST FOR COUNTLESS GENERATIONS.

The Crown Casino in Perth stands as a constant reminder of how and why the city exists. Live fast, die last. Cash rules everything around you.

NOTABLE SPEAKERS

Andrew 'Twiggy' Forrest

Gina Rinehart

Lang Hancock

Kevin Parker

Tim Winton

Heath Ledger

Kim Beazley

Jim Jefferies

almost everything – and penchant for personal watercraft – has wreaked havoc on the Perth Accent.

This polite round dialect, which uses the whole mouth to speak, is rarer than you'd think.

Many believe the approachability of the Perth Accent is part of the reason why so many Perth natives go on to bigger and better things – both here and overseas. No other Western Australian has showcased this quite as well as the late Heath Ledger, whose Perth accent was so unassuming and so easy on the ears that it was palatable to American audiences.

Paul Hogan's character, Crocodile Dundee, spoke with a rounded accent similar to the Perth dialect. Though his was more on the cruder end of the West Australian pronunciation, he wasn't dubbed over either.

In short, the West Australian accent is the least threatening and easiest to understand for a young Betootanese youth, more so than Free Settler or Blackfella. It's also a beautiful part of the country and any young person worth their weight in gidgee should make a beeline for it.

THE MELBOURNE ACC'NT

Spoken almost exclusively in Melbourne, the capital of the People's Republic of Victoria, the Melbourne Acc'nt is somehow breathier than the most puffed out rugby forward, while being as nasal as every Byron Bay folk singer combined.

NOTABLE SPEAKERS

Malcolm Fraser

Molly Meldrum

Bill Lawry

Eddie McGuire

Andrew Bolt

Rupert Murdoch

AREAS

Inner Melbourne

Art galleries in Sydney

Acting schools

The Melbourne Acc'nt was thought to have been introduced to the wider Australian society by former Prime Minister Malcolm Fraser, who learned the elocuted drawl and open-mouthed growl from a pet galah he had as a child.

Holding true to what that influential bird taught him about public speaking, Fraser's accent became synonymous with the Melbourne elite. It was different enough to justify being its own thing – the Melbourne Acc'nt was born.

Out of the seven or so Australian dialects, this one is easily the most distinct.

It can be heard across a room, most frequently an art gallery, as it rises, dips and pauses with a rhythm that sounds both overly irregular and oddly fluent. Similar to Received Pronunciation, spoken by the likes of Malcolm Turnbull and Cate Blanchett, the Melbourne variant sounds more extreme, whereby points and sentences

OUT OF THE SEVEN OR SO AUSTRALIAN DIALECTS, THIS ONE IS EASILY THE MOST DISTINCT.

Melbourne's penchant for European-style political correctness has seen Yarra Creek, which runs through the heart of the city, be classified as both a 'harbour' and a 'river' – when it is clearly just a glorified creek.

are punctuated with hand gestures and a thick growl through a clenched, educated jaw.

They speak as if they're better than you because, in most cases, they are.

However, not everyone in Australia's second-largest city speaks with this accent. Melbourne is a melting pot of creeds, accents and languages. Those who speak with this accent are the Melbournians who speak for a living.

For example, Andrew Bolt's quiet tempered Melbourne voice is similar to Malcolm Fraser's. However, the people to whom Bolt speaks don't speak with a Melbourne Acc'nt. In a recent survey, 9 out of 10 people

who would support Andrew Bolt in a political career either have, or have thought about, throwing rocks at a passing bus or train.

There has yet to be a recorded instance of a person with a Melbourne Acc'nt throwing a rock at a bus.

But there have been many recorded instances of Melbourne-speaking people paying too much for artwork.

In a now infamous incident at the Desert Pea Art Gallery in North Betoota back in 1997, a visiting Toorak woman spent an afternoon walking around the gallery repeating the phrase: 'Simply divine,' although she was saying it without closing

her mouth. Gallery staff had to speak through a translator in order to finalise the transaction. The anonymous lady bought the entire show for close to a quarter of a million dollars, which led to the artist holding the show having a stroke.

To properly handle yourself in Melbourne, when you're about to engage a person in conversation, first inspect their hands and shoes. If they're clean and look expensive, there's a good chance you won't be able to understand what they're saying. If you get lost, speak to the nearest tradesperson or other hi-vis-clad worker.

FREE SETTLER ENGLISH

Most of the time non-threatening, other times very threatening. Speaking softly with an impartial tone is one of the greatest hallmarks of the Free Settler dialect.

The Free Settler Accent, found almost exclusively in Adelaide and other select South Australian enclaves, is subtle at first but once you pick it, you'll hear it everywhere.

Sooner or later, it will stand out. Each time you hear it, you'll look over and see the type of person who didn't descend from a common prisoner.

You'll see a large, swooping forehead and a confident stride. A slight smile delicately written on their face. People from Melbourne might think they're a cut above the rest of the country, but that honour actually lies with the person speaking the Free Settler Dialect.

Much, much rounder than both the Melbourne and Perth accents, when you first hear a proper Adelaide accent, it almost sounds like they're giving a speech. Every single word is pensively laboured over. Each syllable is a well-executed tango. Talk is not cheap in South Australia, so to speak, with purpose and attitude almost a solid necessity.

Thankfully, people who speak with the Free Settler Accent speak slowly. Slowly enough for you, the simple interior savage, to follow. For the Free-Settler purist, some speakers have been observed conversing in Middle English, which was thought to have died out sometime after Shakespeare's death. It's the type of smug faux-Latin pidgin that university professors 'hark the herald' in at the front of the class.

The layperson is not meant to understand what they're saying. That's the point.

Because it's a privilege, not a birthright, to be born with no convict blood flowing through your veins, children born to parents of 'mixed

Above: The ABC is the only network allowed to broadcast in Adelaide because you're least likely to hear a swear word on it.

race' in Adelaide (part convict and part free settler) must have this recorded on their birth certificates. Many of these 'convict muggles' have gone on to become great footballers, and they also speak with the Free Settler Dialect. But no matter how many goals they've kicked, or balls they've rucked, they still won't be fully accepted into the wider South Australian community.

As for what the accent sounds like: give yourself a massive hangover, burn the roof of your mouth with pizza, pop an ice cube into your mouth and speak to your parents.

That's basically it, really.

BECAUSE IT'S A PRIVILEGE, NOT A BIRTHRIGHT, TO BE BORN WITH NO CONVICT BLOOD FLOWING THROUGH YOUR VEINS, CHILDREN BORN TO PARENTS OF 'MIXED RACE' IN ADELAIDE (PART CONVICT AND PART FREE SETTLER) MUST HAVE THIS RECORDED ON THEIR BIRTH CERTIFICATES.

BETOOTANESE PIDGIN

The Betootanese Pidgin is one of the oldest languages in Australia. Its origins can be traced back to the first white settlement of the region in around 1810. Since then, nothing much has changed.

For those of you who are reading this from outside the wider Diamantina region of Queensland, this section could either be quite informative or it could be a total waste of your inner-city time.

The Betootanese Pidgin is one of the oldest non-indigenous languages in Australia. Its origins can be traced back to the first white settlement of the region in around 1810; the English language of the time was still a world away from the ordinary

accent you'd hear today.

Linguists have concluded that elements of the local Aboriginal language are present in Betootan English, as well as a number of languages and dialects of the first European inhabitants. Professor Campbell Alexander-Walsh, from the University of Queensland, has studied Betootan Pidgin as a rank outsider for most of his professional life. In his opinion, it remains one of the most complex and enduring linguistic

anomalies in recorded history.

'You have words with Aboriginal as well as Polish origins. Some sentences are a combination of up to four separate languages, some native, some foreign,' he said.

'For example, you have the traditional, formal greeting of: 'Eyowa yawhichway jooga?' which can be traced back to the Arabic spoken by the Afghan cameleers who populated the region in the 1840s. However, the word 'jooga' has its origins in the Aboriginal language that was, and still is, spoken widely throughout the wider Betoota region. To put it shortly, Betootan Pidgin is not merely its own unique language, it's a fabric of countless languages and slang terms that's simply snowballed through the isolation of the area to become something that's totally detached from the rest of the nation.'

One of the most interesting facets of the language is its use outside the region – most notably on the battlefield. The name code talkers is strongly associated with bilingual Betootan Pidgin speakers, especially recruited during World War II by the Australian Army to serve in their communications units in North Africa and the Pacific. Because Betootan has a complex grammar, it is not nearly mutually intelligible enough with even its closest relatives to provide meaningful information. As it was still an unwritten language, Betootan could satisfy the military requirement for an undecipherable code.

Betootan was spoken only in the Betoota area of South-West Queensland. Its syntax and tonal qualities, not to mention dialects, made it unintelligible to anyone without extensive exposure and training. One estimate indicates that, at the outbreak of World War II, fewer than three non-Betootans could understand the language. However, as the war came to an end, with it came the end of Betootan Pidgin being used outside of Betoota.

'EYOWA YAWHICHWAY JOOGA?'

– HELLO.

'Eyowa yawhichway jooga?' can be traced back to the Arabic spoken by the Afghan cameleers who populated the region in the 1840s.

Photo Credits

BA = Betoota Advocate; PD = public domain; WC = Wikimedia Commons

6 BA; 8 BA; 9 BA; 10–11 BA; 15 BA; 16 WC Bidgee; 17 BA; 18–19 BA; 21 BA; 47 Fran Gibson; 49 Fran Gibson; 51(t) CC G E M; 79(t) Fran Gibson; 80(t) Fran Gibson; 89(b) WC Thennicke; 108–109 WC Thennicke; 111 WC Thennicke; 113 WC jfish92; 115 WC Monkeytypist; 117 WC Peter Campbell; 119 WC Peter Campbell; 121 WC Simon Chamberlain; 123 WC Matt Roberts; 125 WC Michael Coghlan; 126–127 BA; 129 WC Bjenks; 130(t) WC Office of Cory Bernardi; (b) WC Di Bell; 131(t) WC Eva Rinaldi; (b) WC Anonymous9000; 132–133 PD, National Library of New Zealand (23151560); 135 BA; 137 BA; 139(l) WC Mack Male; (r) WC cyclonebill; 140 WC deror_avi; 141 WC V2; 143(l) WC Annette Teng; (c) WC kgbo; (r) Riana Dzasta; 144 WC Brett Jordan; 145 WC BrokenSphere; 147 WC Akabashi; 148 BA; 150–151 WC Patrick Gillet; 153 PD, State Library of NSW (6935 & 43789); 155 WC Naparazzi; 156 BA; 159 WC Patrick Gillet; 161 WC Mobilegnome; 163 Tony Davis; 165 Jayphen; 175 WC Hans Hillewaert; 177 BA; 179 WC Department of Foreign Affairs and Trade; 181(l) BA; (r) Eva Rinaldi; 183 BA; 185 WC JarrahTree; 187 WC Bernard Gagnon; 189 WC orderinchaos; 190 BA

All other photos by Shutterstock.com unless otherwise credited in the caption.

 The ABC 'Wave' device is a trademark of the Australian Broadcasting Corporation and is used under licence by HarperCollins*Publishers* Australia

First published in Australia in 2017
by HarperCollins*Publishers* Australia Pty Limited
ABN 36 009 913 517
harpercollins.com.au

HarperCollins*Publishers*

Level 13, 201 Elizabeth Street, Sydney NSW 2000, Australia
Unit D1, 63 Apollo Drive, Rosedale, Auckland 0632, New Zealand
A 53, Sector 57, Noida, UP, India
1 London Bridge Street, London, SE1 9GF, United Kingdom
2 Bloor Street East, 20th floor, Toronto, Ontario M4W 1A8, Canada
195 Broadway, New York NY 10007, USA

National Library of Australia Cataloguing-in-Publication data:

Betoota's Australia / The Betoota Advocate.
ISBN: 9780733338687 (paperback)
ISBN: 9781460708965 (ebook: epub)
Political satire, Australian.
Popular culture–Humour.
Australian wit and humour.
Newspapers–Sections, columns, etc.
Country life–Queensland.
Other Creators/Contributors: Betoota Advocate.

Cover and internal design by Nick Barclay Designs
Cover images and internal illustrations: Ashley J Nixon
Printed in China by RR Donnelley
The papers used by HarperCollins in the manufacture of this book are a natural, recyclable product made from wood grown in sustainable plantation forests. The fibre source and manufacturing processes meet recognised international environmental standards, and carry certification.